Monasteries of Tibetan Buddhism in China

中国藏传佛教寺庙

Foreign Languages Press Beijing

外 文 出 版 社

Photographer and Writer: Cheng Weidong
Book Project: Lan Peijin
Translator: Yu Ling
English Text Edited by Liang Liangxing
Layout: Yuan Qing
Editor: Lan Peijin

First Edition 2004

Monasteries of Tibetan Buddhism in China

ISBN 7-119-03347-6

© Foreign Languages Press
Published by Foreign Languages Press
24 Baiwanzhuang Road, Beijing 100037, China
Home Page: http://www.flp.com.cn
E-mail Addresses: info@flp.com.cn
                              sales@flp.com.cn
Distributed by China International Book Trading Corporation
35 Chegongzhuang Xilu, Beijing 100044, China
P.O. Box 399, Beijing, China
Printed in the People's Republic of China

Contens 目 录

Foreword

Tibetan Buddhism is one of the three main branches of Chinese Buddhism. With its heartland on the Qinghai-Tibet Plateau, it has a history of more than 1,000 years. In the seventh century, Buddhism spread to the Tubo Kingdom in present-day Tibet from China's Central Plains area and Nepal. It was adopted by the nobility, and later caught on among the common people. The process of its dissemination can be divided into the two periods of "Earlier Propagation of Buddhism" (seventh-ninth centuries i.e. the Tubo period) and the "Later Propagation of Buddhism" (10th-mid 20th centuries). In the second period there was a constant influx of Buddhist masters from India and Nepal to the Qinghai-Tibet Plateau preaching Buddhism. This religion incorporated the indigenous primitive Tibetan religion, Bon, and finally took the shape of Tibetan Buddhism, or what is referred to by the Chinese as Lamaism. Tibetan Buddhism belongs to the Mahayana, or Greater Vehicle, tradition of Buddhism. Its unique feature is the system of reincarnation of holy men.

In the mid-eighth century, during the Earlier Propagation of Buddhism in Tibet, the first Buddhist monastery in Tibetan history—the Samye Monastery—was built in Tibet. The monastery integrated Buddhism's Triratna or three treasures—the Buddha, dharma (law) and Sangha (community of believers)—

A religion followed by many people for generations is a kind of cultural heritage. Tibetan Buddhist art has been passed down for centuries by people like these pilgrims prostrating themselves before the Buddha.

群体的信仰本身就是对一种文化的传承，藏传佛教艺术留传至今，离不开这些一代代磕着长头朝觐的人们。

into one. At the same time, it provided a special site for the study, translation and dissemination of the Buddhist scriptures. The founding of the Samye Monastery was an important milestone in the development of Tibetan Buddhism during the time of the Tubo Kingdom.

Tibetan Buddhism spread into Qinghai, Sichuan, Gansu and Yunnan provinces, and the present-day Inner Mongolia Autonomous Region and Mongolia from the 10th to the 20th centuries during the Later Propagation of Buddhism. Among those who follow Tibetan Buddhism in China are the Tibetan, Mongolian, Yugur, Naxi, Tu and Qiang ethnic groups, in addition to a small number of Han people. Introduced to the royal courts of the Yuan, Ming and Qing dynasties from the 13th century on, Tibetan Buddhism had a considerable influence on imperial policies as regards Tibet and religion. During a long process of historical vicissitudes, social upheavals and changes of dynasty, Tibetan Buddhism became inevitably fused with politics, especially in Tibet, resulting in mutual dependence and complementarity between the two. At the same time, it spread to neighboring countries and regions such as Nepal, Bhutan, Sikkim and Ladakh. The religion also found its way to Europe and America in the early 20th century, where missionary centers or research institutions were set up.

Tibetan Buddhist monasteries and temples were built all over the Qinghai-Tibet Plateau, including in the Yalong Valley in Shannan Prefecture, Amdo in northern Tibet, Qamdo in eastern Tibet, Lhasa in Ü (Anterior Tibet) and Xigaze (Shigatze) in Tsang (Posterior Tibet), as well as at Garze and Aba in Sichuan Province, Deqen in Yunnan Province, Gannan in Gansu Province, some areas inhabited by Tibetans in Qinghai Province and many places in the hinterland.

Well over 4,500 monasteries of various sects of Tibetan Buddhism are included in the historical records, among which, 2,700 were in Tibet, 700 in Qinghai Province, 740 in Sichuan Province, 370 in Gansu Province and 24 in Deqen of Yunnan Province.

In the long development of Tibetan Buddhism, different sects were formed under the influence of different masters, different ways of practice and different scriptures emphasized, as well as different regions and benefactors, although they have all been handed down under the aegis of Esoteric or Tantric Buddhism. There were four major sects in the early period:

of reincarnation of its leaders—the Dalai and Panchen lamas. There are now more than 2,800 monasteries of various sects of Tibetan Buddhism in Tibet and Tibetan-inhabited areas in Qinghai, Gansu, Sichuan and Yunnan provinces (not including Inner Mongolia and other places in the hinterland), among which 1,460— half of the total number—belong to the Gelug, or Yellow, Sect.

Gelug means a "virtuous, good disciple." Following both the Esoteric and Exoteric disciplines of Buddhism, the Gelug Sect stresses full respect for monastic discipline and adheres to a systematic study of the Buddhist tenets. As its founder Tsongkhapa wore a yellow hat during the formative years of the sect and his followers adopted that fashion, the Gelug Sect was also popularly known as the Yellow Hat Sect, or the Yellow Sect for short.

Tsongkhapa, Lozang Drakpa (1357-1419), was born in present-day Huangzhong County, Qinghai Province. He was initiated into monkhood at the age of seven, and nine years later went to Tibet to study under masters of all the schools of Tibetan Buddhism. Gradually, he formed his own religious doctrinal system, and became the founder of the Gelug Sect

Monks painting a mandala (circular or square altar).
僧人们用色粉绘制坛城。

of Tibetan Buddhism. He is a great figure in Tibetan history, as a noted philosopher, thinker and religious reformer. In 1409, Tsongkhapa established the Ganden Monastery in Lhasa. He oversaw the building of the Drepung Monastery on the western outskirts of Lhasa in 1416, and the Sera Monastery on the northern outskirts of Lhasa in 1418. In 1447, Tsongkhapa's disciple Gedun Truppa built the Tashilhunpo Monastery in Xigaze, which later became the residence of the Panchen Lamas. In 1577, in memory of Tsongkhapa the Kumbum Monastery was built in Huangzhong County, the hometown of Tsongkhapa. In 1710, the first reincarnation of the Jamyang Lama built the Labrang Monastery in

Nyingma, Kadam, Sakya and Kagyu. The latter was further divided into the Shangpa Kagyu and Dakpo Kagyu sub-sects. In the early 15th century, Tsongkhapa initiated religious reform, and, on the basis of the doctrine of the Kadam Sect, established the Gelug Sect, which was also known as the New Kadam Sect. Subsequently, the Kadam Sect disappeared from areas inhabited by the Tibetans, and the Gelug Sect became the mainstream representing Tibetan Buddhism. The Gelug Sect instituted a system

Buddhist images and mantras are often seen carved on cliffs and stones along pilgrim roads.
朝圣的路上常常可以见到这些刻在山崖、路边石头上的佛像、六字真言等。

Gannan, Gansu Province. Both monasteries have since been very influential among the Buddhist believers in Gansu, Qinghai and Sichuan provinces, and the Gelug Sect has become the most widespread and influential school of Tibetan Buddhism.

The Nyingma Sect is the second-biggest Tibetan Buddhist sect next to the Gelug Sect. Nyingma means "ancient," and the sect mainly follows the tradition of Esoteric Buddhism. As its monks wore, and still wear, red hats and robes, this sect was popularly known as the Red Hat Sect, or simply the Red Sect. It was the earliest sect formed by incorporating the Esoteric School of Buddhism with the indigenous Bonism. The sect had no monastery nor any systematic doctrines of its own in the early stage, as it was taught secretly and individually. It was not until the 11th century that the sect came into its own, when it had begun to have its own monasteries and gradually formed its sutras. The formal founder of the sect at that time was the Indian Tantric adept Padmasambhava. The Nyingma Sect now has more than 750 monasteries in Tibet and Tibetan-inhabited areas in Qinghai, Gansu, Sichuan and Yunnan provinces. In the 14th century the sect spread to Bhutan and Nepal. In modern times, it has built monasteries in India, Belgium, Greece and the United States, and has published its scriptures in these countries.

The Kagyu Sect was one of the early Tibetan Buddhist sects. Kagyu in Tibetan means "to carry forward or teach the Buddha's doctrine." One of the important features of the Kagyu Sect is that its tenets are transmitted orally. It is said that in the early period the founding master of the sect wore a white robe while preaching, so the sect was, and still is, also known as the "White Sect." There are at present some 360 monasteries belonging to the Kagyu Sect, located mostly in Tibet and Yushu in Qinghai Province.

Monks blowing *suona* horns at the Monlam Prayer Festival in Lhasa.
大法会上吹唢呐的僧人。

Founded in the 11th century, the Sakya Sect was one of the four most influential Buddhist sects in Tibetan history. It is also known as the "Striped Sect" because of the red, white and black stripes symbolizing Manjusri, Avalokitesvara (Goddess of Mercy) and Vajrapani, the Lord of Secrets, painted on the walls of the major monastery of the sect—the Sakya Monastery. Sakya means "gray-white earth" in Tibetan, implying good luck. The sect was founded on the basis of the Exoteric and Esoteric Buddhist doctrines of Lamdre and Margaphala—the teachings that describe the stages along the path to enlightenment. Its founders were the Five Forefathers of the Sakya. There are now over 140 monasteries of the Sakya Sect, mostly in Tibet, with the Sakya Monastery as the most famous.

Other branches of Tibetan Buddhism include the Kadam, Shiche, and Joyul, which have all gone out of the picture as religious sects on the Qinghai-Tibet Plateau, although their doctrines are still popular in Tibetan areas.

Tibetan Buddhism, with its long history and brilliant culture, has become an important religion that has had a profound influence not only in China but also worldwide. In addition to the monasteries belonging to the Tibetan Buddhist sects mentioned above, there are also many other Buddhist temples and monasteries scattered around China that are still as magnificent as they were in the past. They include the

Scriptures preserved in a monastery.
寺庙内收藏的经书

earliest Tibetan Buddhist temple — the Trandruk Temple in Shannan Prefecture. In addition, there are the Champa Ling, the largest Gelug Sect monastery in eastern Tibet, built by Tsongkhapa's disciple; the Lama Ling, the Red Sect monastery in Nyingchi; the Toling Monastery at Zanda in Ngari built during the Guge Kingdom almost 1,000 years ago; the Shalu Monastery in Xigaze Prefecture; the Pelkor Chode Monastery in Gyangze County; the Tsurpu Monastery in Doilungdeqen County; the Potala Palace, Jokhang Temple and Ramoche Temple in Lhasa; the Litang Chamchen Chokhor Monastery in the Tibetan Autonomous Prefecture of Garze in Sichuan Province; the Songtsen Ling in the Tibetan Autonomous Prefecture of Deqen in Yunnan Province; the Yonghegong Lamasery and the Xihuangsi Temple in Beijing; the Wudangzhao Monastery in the Inner Mongolia Autonomous Region; and the eight outlying temples surrounding the Imperial Summer Resort in Chengde, Hebei Province. These are only a few representatives of the myriad of Tibetan Buddhist monasteries. Some of them might not belong to a specific sect, while others might incorporate features from various Tibetan Buddhist sects. There are some monasteries belonging to another sect in name, but actually have long been influenced and assimilated by the

Gelug Sect. Some temples, like those on Mount Wutai in Shanxi Province, belong to the Han-Chinese Buddhist tradition, but have acquired features of Tibetan

Murals in Tibetan Buddhist monasteries, with a wide range of subjects, display superb craftsmanship.
藏传佛教寺庙内壁画的内容极为广泛，画工也十分精湛。

Buddhist monasteries. These monasteries, while contributing greatly to the recording and preservation of history, and the spreading of culture, have attained very high artistic levels in the aspects of architecture, painting and sculpture. They are the most precious historical and cultural treasures the Tibetans and people of other ethnic groups living on the Qinghai-Tibet Plateau have bequeathed to mankind.

The Monlam is one of the most important Buddhist festivals in Tibet.
拉萨祈祷大法会是西藏重要的佛事活动之一。

前　言

藏传佛教是中国佛教三大系之一，它以青藏高原为主要传播地区。据考证至今已有 1000 多年历史。公元 7 世纪，佛教先后从中国的中原地区和尼泊尔传入当时的吐蕃，先是在王公贵族中间流行，后来逐步传到了民间。其传播的过程分为"前弘期"（公元 7 世纪——9 世纪，即吐蕃时期）和"后弘期"（公元 10 世纪——20 世纪中叶）。在"后弘期"漫长的历史进程中，不断有印度和尼泊尔等地的佛教高僧前往青藏高原传法，同时也吸收和融汇了西藏本土固有的原始宗教——本教，最终形成了属于大乘佛教的藏语系佛教——藏传佛教，汉语俗称"喇嘛教"。独特的活佛转世制度是该佛教一大特点。

在藏传佛教传播的前弘期，公元 8 世纪中叶，西藏历史上吐蕃建起了第一座集佛、法、僧三位于一体的佛教寺院——桑耶寺，该寺的建立不仅使当时吐蕃王朝有了一个"三宝"齐全的正规宗教活动中心，同时成为传播、学习、翻译佛经的专门场所。桑耶寺的建立，是藏传佛教在吐蕃时期发展进程中的一个重要里程碑。

藏传佛教于后弘期开始传入青海、四川、甘肃、内蒙、云南，以及今蒙古共和国，在中国信奉藏传佛教的有藏、蒙、裕固、纳西、土、羌等民族，汉族中也有少数信奉者。13 世纪后传入元、明、清宫廷，对中央政府的治藏政策和宗教政策产生了重大影响。在漫长的发展过程中，由于历史变迁，社会动荡，朝代更迭，使藏传佛教与政治势力自然地紧密结合在

Masks used in Tibetan opera are developed from those used in Tibetan shamanist rites.
藏戏中的面具是由藏族原始巫舞和寺庙跳神驱鬼面具的基础上发展而来的。

一起，于是教依政而行，政依教而立，政教相互依存。政教结合的社会制度与环境给藏传佛教的复兴与发展创造了更加宽松的外部条件。藏传佛教由宫廷走向民间逐渐成为了平民自由信仰的宗教。此间，日趋强盛的藏传佛教还先后渗透传入尼泊尔、不丹、锡金、拉达克等周边邻国及邻境，20 世纪初又开始传入欧美并在这些地区分别建起了传教中心或传教研究机构。

伴随着藏传佛教的广泛传播和深入发展，为宏扬佛法，在雪域高原的广大区域，包括西藏山南雅砻河谷、藏北安多、藏

The Nyingma Sect of Tibetan Buddhism has become known as the "Red Sect," because its monks wear red hats and robes.
藏传佛教中的宁玛派。此派僧人因着红色衣冠，故俗称"红教"。

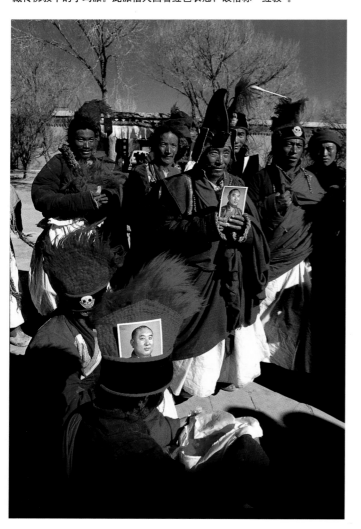

东昌都、前藏拉萨、后藏日喀则，以及四川的甘孜、阿坝，云南迪庆、甘肃甘南、青海的部分藏区和内地诸多地区广泛修建寺庙、佛殿等宗教场所，从而使藏传佛教在广大藏区及内地的传播和发展有了更加深厚的社会基础和保障。

据调查，历史上，整个西藏地区及青海、甘肃、四川和云南部分藏区曾有藏传佛教各宗派寺院共约4500多座，其中西藏有2700多座，青海约700多座，四川740多座，甘肃370多座，云南迪庆24座。

藏传佛教在漫长的发展过程中，虽以密教付法传承为根本，但因不同师承、不同修持教授、所据不同经典和对经典的不同理解等佛教内部诸因素，以及不同地域、不同施主等佛教外部因素又形成了众多派别。这些派别主要有宁玛派、噶当派、萨迦派、噶举派等前期四大派，其中噶举派又分为香巴噶举和塔波噶举两大系统。15世纪初，宗喀巴对宗教进行了改革，在继承噶当派教法基础上，创立了最有影响的格鲁派，又叫"新噶当派"，而曾作为独立宗派的噶当派，从此就在藏族地区消失了，格鲁派成为了藏传佛教各教派中最有代表性的主流教派。该派后来形成达赖和班禅两大活佛体系。目前，据了解在整个西藏，以及青海、甘肃、四川和云南等部分藏区（不包括内蒙及内地其它地区）现有藏传佛教各宗派寺院共约2800余座，其中格鲁派黄教寺庙就有1460多座，占了藏传佛教各宗派寺院总数二分之一。

"格鲁"意为善规，该派显宗、密宗并重，主张僧人应以严守戒律和修习次第为本。因创始人宗喀巴在创教期间头戴黄色桃型僧帽和该派僧人在法会上多戴此帽而俗称"黄帽派"或"黄教"。宗喀巴·洛桑札巴（1357－1419），生于安多宗喀地区，即今青海省湟中县。他7岁出家，16岁赴西藏广拜名师，学法深造，逐渐形成了自己的宗教思想体系，不仅成为藏传佛教格鲁派的创立者，还成为一位著名的哲学家、思想家和宗教改革家，是藏族历史上的一位伟大人物。1409年，宗喀巴在拉萨建立了著名的甘丹寺，1416年，他命弟子在拉萨西郊修建了哲蚌寺，1418年，其弟子强钦曲杰又在拉萨北效修建了色拉寺。拉萨三大寺的建立，既为格鲁派黄教奠定了重要的发展基础，也成为佛教信徒向往的朝佛圣地。1447年，宗喀巴弟子根敦珠巴在后藏日喀则又修建了扎什伦布寺，该寺后来成为历世班禅大师的驻锡地。为纪念宗喀巴大师，1577年在其诞生地青海湟中修建了塔尔寺，1710年第一世嘉木样活佛在甘肃甘南修建拉卜楞寺，这些规模宏大的寺庙，在甘、青、川等藏区广大信教群众中产生了巨大的影响。从此，格鲁派黄教逐渐成为藏传佛教以及藏族社会上分布最广、势力最大、影响最深远的一大宗派。

宁玛派，是仅次于格鲁派而位居第二的藏传佛教另一大宗派。"宁玛"一词意为"古"或"旧"，以传承弘扬旧密法为主。该派僧人均著红色衣冠，故俗称"红教"或"红帽派"。它是传入西藏的密宗吸收了当地本教内容而形成的最早教派。由于宁玛派在早期采取秘密单独传授的方式，所以没有寺院僧侣组织和构成教派的系统教义。到了11世纪后才开始有了红教寺庙，并逐步有了自己教派的经典，而正式形成为一个教派，尊莲花生为祖师。该派现在西藏、青海、甘肃、四川和云南藏区共有750多座寺院。14世纪宁玛派就传播到不丹、尼泊尔；近代，印度、比利时、希腊、美国等都建有寺庙并出版了教义著作。

噶举派，是藏传佛教的宗派之一，藏语"噶"字意为"佛语"，"举"字则为"传承"。"噶举"意为教谕或教传，师徒相承，口语传授，耳听心会，注重密法，不重经典。口耳相传是该教派的重要特征之一。相传该派师祖早年修法时，身穿白色僧衣，故称"白教"。噶举派现拥有360多座寺院，以西藏

A distant view of the Potala Palace. (Photo by Wang Chunshu)
远眺布达拉宫。（王春树 摄）

和青海玉树为该派两大活动区域。

萨迦派，是藏传佛教四大教派中曾有着重要历史地位和影响的一个重要派别，创始于11世纪。因其主寺萨迦寺围墙涂有象征文殊、观音、金刚手菩萨的红、白、黑三色花条，故俗称"花教"。"萨迦"，藏语意为灰白色的土地，寓意为吉祥之土。该派以道果法等显密教法为教理体系而自成一派，历史上最有代表性的就是著名的萨迦五祖。萨迦派现有寺院140多座，其势力主要在西藏境内，以萨迦寺为代表。除以上各派外，在藏传佛教中，尚有诸如噶当派、希解派、觉域派等，目前只是以宗派学说的形式在藏区流行，而作为一种宗派实体在青藏高原几乎已不存在了。

有着悠久历史和灿烂文化的藏传佛教，随着时代的发展与历史的变迁，目前已成为中国乃至世界范围有着十分重要地位和具有深远影响的宗教派别。藏传佛教各宗派中，除上述所提及的寺庙外，各地还有不少佛殿、庙宇和寺院，它们不仅昔日辉煌荣耀，如今仍光芒依旧。诸如：西藏最早建立的佛殿——山南昌珠寺；由宗喀巴弟子所建的藏东最大黄教寺庙——强巴林寺；林芝地区的红教寺庙——喇嘛林寺；与古格王国同期的——阿里扎达托林寺；后藏日喀则地区的夏鲁寺和江孜白居寺；堆龙德庆境内的楚布寺；拉萨市内的布达拉宫、大昭寺、小昭寺；四川甘孜藏族自治州的长青春科尔寺；云南迪庆藏族自治州的松赞林寺；内地名寺还有北京的雍和宫、西黄寺；内蒙古的五当召；河北承德避暑山庄的外八庙等等。这些寺庙虽然只是众多藏传佛教寺庙中的部分代表，而它们其中有的还不归属任何一个派别，有的融各教派为一寺，有的名义上仍属某个宗派，而实际却早已被格鲁派黄教渗透、异化。还有的寺庙整体上虽然归属汉传佛教，但其中相当部分却具有藏传佛教寺庙的特点，如山西五台山的一些寺庙等等。但这些寺庙在记录、传播、收藏历史文化方面作出了重要的贡献，寺庙本身在建筑、绘画、雕塑等艺术方面达到了极高的水平，它们在藏传佛教的历史上乃至今天同样都有着极其重要的地位，是青藏高原聪明智慧的藏民族和其他各民族人民共同留给人类最珍贵的历史文化宝藏。

1. Prayer flags fluttering over a mountain pass on the Qinghai-Tibet Plateau.
耸立在高原山口的经幡。

The Potala Palace 布达拉宫

The Potala Palace on the Red Hill in Lhasa, capital of the Tibet Autonomous Region, was built by King Songtsen Gampo of Tubo in the seventh century to welcome his bride Princess Wencheng of the Tang imperial house. After being renovated many times over the centuries, it is now the largest and most intact palace complex in Tibet. Potala, in Sanskrit, means "Sacred Place of the Goddess of Mercy." The palace was used as the winter residence of the Dalai Lamas. Built entirely from wood and stone, the principal structure of the palace is 13 stories, or 115 m, high. The White Palace was completed in 1645, after three years of construction, under the supervision of the Fifth Dalai Lama, and the Red Palace was built in 1690, during the reign of Emperor Kangxi of the Qing Dynasty. The Potala Palace is not only a paradigm of traditional Tibetan architecture, but also a museum of art treasures and precious cultural relics. In its collection are title-conferring edicts from em-perors of the Ming and Qing dynasties, gold seals bestowed by emperors, gold decrees, jade decrees, gold plaques, gifts, ancient Tibetan records, statues of Buddhas, murals, thangka religious icons, articles of tribute and Buddhist ritual objects. The Potala Palace was added to UNESCO's World Cultural Heritage List in 1994.

位于西藏拉萨市内的玛布日山上，初建于公元7世纪，是吐蕃赞普松赞干布为迎娶唐文成公主而建，后经历代整修，成为西藏最大、最完整的宫堡式建筑群。"布达拉"，梵语意为观世音圣地，为历代达赖喇嘛的冬宫。布达拉宫依山而建，1645年在五世达赖喇嘛主持下，历时3年建成白宫，康熙二十九年（1690年）又修建了红宫。布达拉宫主楼共13层，高115米，全部为石木结构。布达拉宫不仅是藏式建筑的典范，还是艺术精品和珍贵文物的博物馆，宫内不仅藏有明清帝王的封诏、印鉴、金册、玉册、金匾、礼品，还藏有众多藏文典籍、佛像、唐卡、法器、贡品等无以记数。1994年被联合国教科文组织列入世界文化遗产名录。

2. 3. The Potala Palace—a holy place
in the snowland of Tibet.
雪域圣殿—布达拉宫。

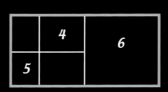

4. Painted sculptures in the West Hall.
西大殿框梁彩塑装饰。

5. The Hall of Maitreya, the Buddha of the Future.
强巴佛殿。

6. One of the stupa halls in the Potala Palace.
灵塔殿之一。

7. The mandala altars in the Kalachakra (Wheel of Time) Hall.
时轮佛殿内的密宗坛城。

8. The pilgrims' circumambulation path below the Potala Palace.
布达拉宫下的转经路。

The Jokhang Temple 大昭寺

The Jokhang Temple, located in the center of Lhasa, was first built in the mid-seventh century. It is one of the most magnificent buildings dating from the Tubo Kingdom period. Architecturally this 25,000-sq-m monastery is a combination of Tibetan and Han-Chinese styles. Housed in the monastery are innumerable precious cultural relics, including Buddhist statues, scriptures, murals, sculptures and Buddhist ritual objects. With a life-size statue of 12-year-old Sakyamuni brought to Tibet by the Tang-Dynasty Princess Wencheng, the monastery became a magnet for Buddhist pilgrims and a center of religious activities. Therefore, it was well maintained, renovated and expanded by all Tibetan Buddhist sects in every historical period, and became a holy palace honored by all sects of Tibetan Buddhism. On November 29, 1995, a grand ceremony to determine the sacred reincarnation of the 10th Panchen Lama was held before the statue of Sakyamuni in the Jokhang Temple. In accordance with religious rituals and historical conventions, the 11th Panchan Erdeni Chokyi Gyalpo was determined by drawing lots from a gold urn. The Jokhang Temple has applied for inclusion on UNESCO's World Cultural Heritage List.

位于拉萨市中心，占地 2.5 万平方米，始建于 7 世纪中叶，是西藏现存吐蕃时期最辉煌的建筑之一，藏语全称 "惹萨垂朗祖拉康"，意为 "羊土神变经堂"，相传由山羊驮土填湖而建。寺庙融汉藏两种建筑风格于一体。内藏有佛像、经书、壁画、雕塑、法器等珍贵文物宝藏无数。由于寺内供奉唐文成公主入藏时带来的释迦牟尼 12 岁等身佛像，而成为藏传佛教朝圣之地和重要活动中心。在各历史时期，该寺都受到藏传佛教各教派供养、维修和扩建，因此，大昭寺实际已无宗派界线而成为藏传佛教各教派共同供奉的一座圣殿。1995 年 11 月 29 日，举世瞩目的第十世班禅大师转世灵童认定仪典就在该寺释迦牟尼佛祖像前隆重举行，按照宗教仪轨和历史定制，经金瓶掣签认定了第十一世班禅额尔德尼·确吉杰布。目前，大昭寺正在申报世界文化遗产名录。

	10
9	

9. The Jokhang Temple, located in the center of Lhasa.
   位于拉萨市中心的大昭寺。

10. The life-size statue of Sakyamuni enshrined in the central hall of the Jokhang Temple.
    释迦牟尼12岁等身佛像供奉在该寺中心殿堂。

11. The Tang-Tubo [Han-Tibetan] Alliance Monument, erected in 823, during the Tang Dynasty, still stands in the square in front of the temple.
寺前的《唐蕃会盟碑》立于公元 823 年。

12. The golden roofs of the Jokhang Temple.
大昭寺金顶。

13. On November 29, 1995, a grand ceremony to determine the sacred reincarnation of the 10th Panchen was held before the statue of Sakyamuni in the Jokhang Temple.
1995 年 11 月 29 日，第十世班禅转世灵童金瓶掣签认定仪典在该寺释迦牟尼佛祖像前隆重举行。

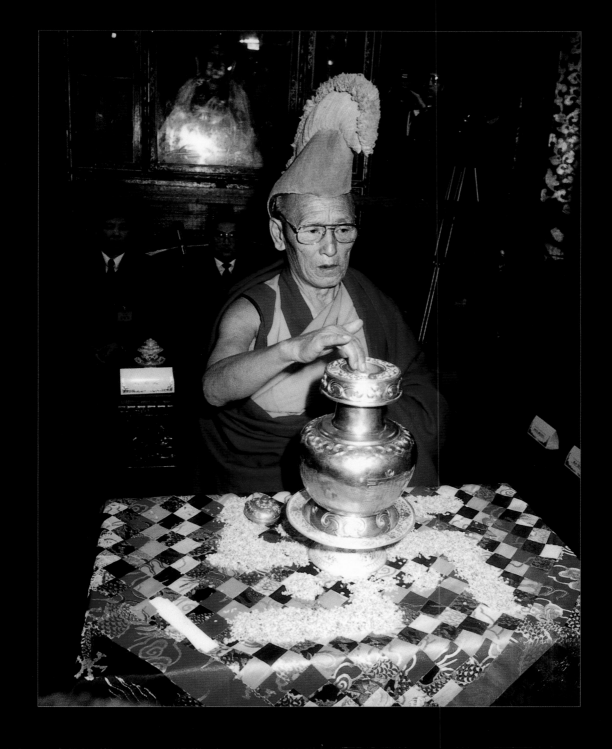

14. The gold urn, a gift from the Qing Emperor Qianlong, used for drawing lots to determine the reincarnation of the Panchen Lama, is preserved in the Jokhang Temple.

1792年清乾隆皇帝赐给西藏,用于活佛转世掣签之用的金苯巴瓶之一藏于该寺内。

15. The 11th Panchen Erdeni Chokyi Gyalpo (center) was confirmed after drawing lots from a gold urn.

经金瓶掣签认定的第十一世班禅额尔德尼·确吉杰布。

16. The annual Monlam Prayer Festival, started by Tsongkhapa, founder of the Gelug Sect, has been held for centuries at the Jokhang Temple. The photo shows a *gekor* ("iron pole monk"), whose duty is to maintain order on the occasion.

格鲁派创始人宗喀巴创立的拉萨祈祷大法会（又称传召）始于大昭寺，一年一度延续至今。图为法会中的铁棒喇嘛。

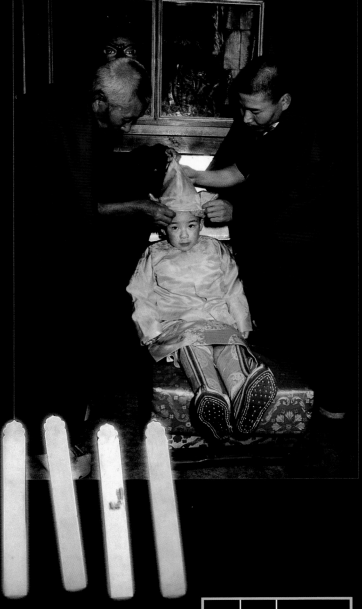

	15	16
14		

17. Debating is an important part of the Monlam Prayer Festival. The monks are tested through debates and arguments for a theological degree.
辩经是大法会的重要内容，这是考取学位的喇嘛正在进行辩经。

18. Monks blow conch shells, which are symbols of auspiciousness.
寺内僧人吹起吉祥的法螺。

19. Worshippers before the Jokhang Temple.
在大昭寺前朝拜的人们。

The Ramoche Temple 小昭寺

The Ramoche Temple is located one km north of the Jokhang Temple in Lhasa. Built in the same period as the Jokhang Temple, it was a well-known Buddhist temple in the early years of the Tubo Kingdom, and later became the site of the Upper Tantric College—one of the colleges of Tantric or Esoteric Buddhism of the Gelug Sect. In this temple of 2,100 sq m, there is a bronze-and-gold statue of Acala, a leading Bodhisattva of Esoteric Buddhism. The statue was brought to Tibet by the Nepalese princess Trisun. It is a destination for both pilgrims and tourists.

位于大昭寺北约1公里处，藏文全称"甲达惹木切拉康"，汉语称小昭寺。小昭寺与大昭寺同时修建，为吐蕃早期著名佛寺，后为格鲁派密宗经院之一的上密院所在地。该寺占地2100多平方米，寺内主供尼泊尔赤尊公主入藏带来的不动金刚鎏金铜佛像（释迦牟尼佛），现为僧众朝圣和旅游圣地。

20. The ancient Ramoche Temple in Lhasa.
    拉萨古寺——小昭寺。
21. The bronze-and-gold statue of Acala
    enshrined in the temple.
    该寺主供的不动金刚鎏金佛像（释迦牟尼佛）。
22. A Buddhist service held in the Ramoche
    Temple.
    寺内举行佛事活动。

	21	
20		22

The Ganden Monastery 甘丹寺

Located in Dagze County 45 km east of Lhasa, the Ganden Monastery was the first monastery founded in 1409 by Tsongkhapa, founder of the Gelug Sect of Tibetan Buddhism. The oldest of the three great monasteries in Lhasa (the other two being the Drepung and Sera monasteries), it also ranks first of the six great Gelug Sect monasteries of Tibetan Buddhism.

Ganden in the Tibetan language means "glorious land." In January 1409, by the Tibetan calendar, Tsongkhapa inaugurated the first Monlam Prayer Festival in the Jokhang Temple in memory of Sakyamuni, during which he advocated religious reform and the revival of Buddhism in Tibet. Then he supervised the building of the Ganden Monastery, and became its first abbot. The initiation of the Monlam Prayer Festival and the building of the Ganden Monastery marked the formal founding of a new sect of Tibetan Buddhism—the Gelug Sect. Tsongkhapa lived in the monastery from its establishment until he passed away on October 25, 1419 by the Tibetan calendar. This monastery became the major place for teaching, learning, and practicing the tenets of the Gelug Sect. The Ganden Monastery is most famous for a stupa where the remains of Tsongkhapa are preserved, and a silver stupa containing the remains of all the abbots of the monastery after him. On the 25th day of the 10th month by the Tibetan calendar, the Festival of Lamps is celebrated every year to commemorate the death of Tsongkhapa. During the "cultural revolution" (1966-1976), the monastery was badly damaged, but many of the buildings have been restored and expanded.

位于拉萨市东45公里处的达孜县境内，是藏传佛教格鲁派创始人宗喀巴于1409年创建的第一座格鲁派寺院，它与其相继修建的哲蚌寺、色拉寺合称拉萨三大寺，是中国藏传佛教格鲁派六大寺庙之一。因该寺是宗喀巴创建、升座和圆寂之地，因而其宗教地位居格鲁派各寺之首。

甘丹寺，藏语全称"卓噶丹朗巴杰卧林"，意为"喜足尊胜洲"。1409年藏历元月，宗喀巴在拉萨大昭寺成功首创纪念释迦牟尼祈愿法会，改革宗教，振兴佛法，随后就修建了甘丹寺并成为该寺首任法台。法会和建寺标志着藏传佛教一个新的教派 — 格鲁派的正式形成。自甘丹寺建成，至1419年藏历10月25日宗喀巴圆寂，宗喀巴常住此寺，所以这里又是格鲁派的根本道场。该寺最著名的当属宗喀巴大师的肉身灵塔以及藏有该寺历代法台（主持）的银质灵塔。每年藏历10月25日，该寺都要隆重举行传统的"燃灯节"，纪念宗喀巴大师。"文化大革命"中，该寺破坏严重，现部分得到修复和扩建。

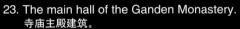

23. The main hall of the Ganden Monastery.
    寺庙主殿建筑。
24. The thrones of reincarnated lamas.
    殿内活佛宝座。
25. A hall of the Ganden Monastery.
    寺内佛殿一角。
26. Details of a mural in the Ganden Monastery.
    甘丹寺壁画局部。

		25	
23	24		26

27. The Ganden Monastery, one of the six great monasteries of the Gelug Sect of Tibetan Buddhism.

藏传佛教格鲁派六大寺庙之一的甘丹寺。

The Drepung Monastery 哲蚌寺

Situated at the foot of Gepel Wutse Hill five km northwest of Lhasa, the Drepung Monastery was built in 1416, during the Ming Dynasty, under the supervision of Jamyang Choje, a leading disciple of Tsongkhapa. With an area of 250,000 sq m, it is one of the six great monasteries of the Gelug Sect of Tibetan Buddhism. Drepung means "heaps of rice." The buildings of the monastery are mostly white, looking in the distance like rice heaped up on the mountain. The full name of the monastery in the Tibetan language—Pelden Drepung Chogle Nampar Gyalwa Ling—means "a lucky continent esteemed by all for the accumulation of rice." The monastery is composed of the Tsochen Hall, which can seat 7,000 monks, four Dratsang or monastic colleges, and the Ganden Photrang. As the second to the fifth Dalai Lamas lived in the Ganden Photrang before the Potala Palace was renovated and expanded, the Drepung Monastery was once the center of the Gelug Sect and a synonym for the theocratic government. The monastery has an extensive collection of treasures and cultural relics. Well-known for its deep and serene stone lanes, cloisters, imposing halls, and row upon row of towers and pavilions, the monastery is also referred to as a "museum of monastic stone inscriptions" for the numerous Buddhist stone statues in it and in the nearby valley. The famous Buddha painting unfolding ceremony held in the Drepung Monastery is the traditional opening as well as the most important and impressive part of the Shodon (Yogurt) Festival, which attracts almost all the residents of Lhasa every year.

位于拉萨市西北5公里的更培乌孜山下，占地25万平方米。明永乐十四年（1416年），宗喀巴著名弟子降央曲结受师命创建，是藏传佛教格鲁派六大寺庙之一。藏文全称"贝曲哲蚌确唐门杰勒朗巴杰瓦林"，意为"吉祥米聚十方尊胜州"。"哲蚌"意为"堆积大米"，因该寺建筑以白色为主调，远望如同大米堆积山腰，故取名哲蚌寺。该寺内藏珍宝文物无数，由可容纳7000名僧众诵经礼佛的措钦大殿和四大扎仓，以及甘丹颇章等几部分组成。在布达拉宫修复以前，从第二至第五世达赖喇嘛都住在该寺内的甘丹颇章，从而使这里一度成为当时格鲁派的统治中心和政教合一政权的代称。整个寺庙不仅以幽深的石巷、回廊、巍峨的殿宇及栉比的楼阁著称，同时寺外山谷内众多造型各异的石刻佛像，也是该寺一大特色，人称"寺庙石刻博物馆"。著名的哲蚌寺展佛，几乎令拉萨万人空巷，成为每年一度的拉萨雪顿节传统序幕和最重要、隆重的活动之一。

28. Stone statues of the Buddha in the valley near the Drepung Monastery.
寺外遍及山谷的石刻佛像。

29. The major hall of the Drepung Monastery
寺庙主殿外景。

A view of the Drepung Monastery.

30. 寺庙一角。

The Drepung Monastery, one of the six

31. great monasteries of the Gelug Sect o Tibetan Buddhism.
藏传佛教格鲁派六大寺庙之一哲蚌寺。

32

32. The traditional Buddha painting unfolding ceremony held in the Drepung Monastery is one of the most important parts of the annual Shodon (Yogurt) Festival.

哲蚌寺展佛是拉萨每年雪顿节的最重要传统内容之一。

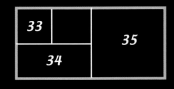

33. A mural in the Drepung Monastery.
   哲蚌寺壁画。
34. Monks of a Dratsang or monastic college in the Drepung Monastery.
   哲蚌寺佛学院的僧人。
35. The sculptured gateway to the main hall of the Drepung Monastery.
   寺庙主殿大门建筑雕塑。

The Sera Monastery 色拉寺

Situated at the foot of Sera Wutse Hill three km north of Lhasa, the Sera Monastery was built in 1418 by Chanchen Choje, another disciple of Tsongkhapa. One of the three large monasteries in Lhasa, it is also one of the six great Tibetan Buddhist monasteries of the Gelug Sect. Tsongkhapa passed away right after the Sera Monastery was completed. Sera in the Tibetan language means "wild rose." Sera Wutse Hill is said to be covered with wild roses when the monastery was completed, and the full name of the monastery in Tibetan means "Sera Mahayana Continent." At its height the monastery was populated by nearly 10,000 monks, with more than 100 "Living Buddhas" of different status. The renowned Hutuktus (a title bestowed by the Qing court on Living Buddhas) such as Reting, Tsomo Ling and Phapalha, all came from this monastery.

Among the vast quantities of cultural relics housed here the well-preserved murals on many buildings are noteworthy. A grand Buddha painting unfolding ceremony is also held in the Sera Monastery at the opening of the Shodon (Yogurt) Festival in Lhasa every year.

位于拉萨城北3公里处的色拉乌孜山麓，为宗喀巴弟子强钦曲杰遵照师命于1418年始建的拉萨三大寺中最后建成的一座寺庙，也是藏传佛教格鲁派六大寺庙之一。但该寺刚建成，宗喀巴就圆寂了。色拉寺藏语全称"色拉泰钦林"，意为"色拉大乘洲"。色拉，藏语意为"野玫瑰"，相传此山遍地长满野玫瑰，寺建成后便得此名。该寺兴盛时期僧人近万，大小活佛上百。著名的热振、策墨林、帕巴拉等呼图克图均属该寺僧籍。寺内藏有珍宝无数，许多建筑的壁画大多保持了原貌，每年拉萨雪顿节开幕当天，这里也举行盛大的展佛活动。

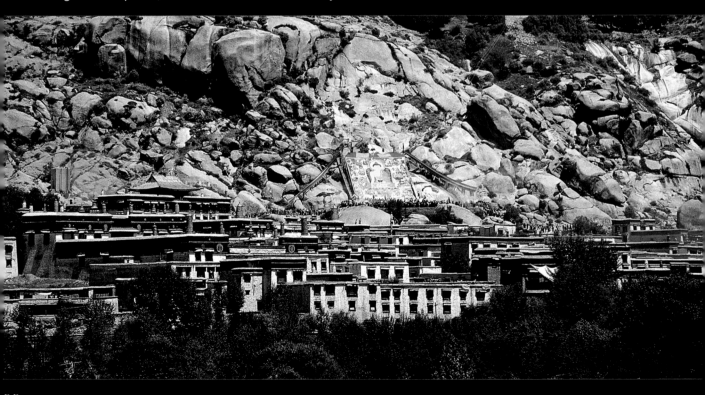

36. The Sera Monastery, one of the six great monasteries of the Gelug Sect of Tibetan Buddhism.
藏传佛教格鲁派六大寺庙之 —— 色拉寺。

37. The annual Buddha painting unfolding ceremony held in the Sera Monastery attracts a large number of pilgrims and tourists.
每年一度的色拉寺展佛都会吸引众多的信教群众和游人。

38. Part of the Sera Monastery.
色拉寺一角。

	37	
36		38

39. Refined and lifelike sculptures in the Sera Monastery.
寺庙精美生动的建筑雕塑。

40. The flagpole in front of the major hall of the Sera Monastery is a symbol of dignity and good fortune.
寺庙主殿前象征威严和吉祥的大风马旗杆。

41. Details of a mural in the Sera Monastery.
色拉寺壁画局部。

42. Stone Buddhist statues in the Sera Monastery.
寺内石刻佛像。

Situated in Lhasa's Doilungdeqen County, the Tsurpu Monastery was established by Dusum Khyenpa, a disciple of Dakpo Lhaje (founder of the Dakpo Kagyu Sect of Tibetan Buddhism), in 1189. It is the major monastery of the Karma Kagyu (Black Hat) Sect, one of the four sub-sects of the Dakpo Kagyu Sect. The monastery has been highly regarded in and outside China as the birthplace of the system of reincarnation of a great lama after his death, a feature unique to Tibetan Buddhism.

位于西藏拉萨市堆龙德庆县境内，该寺1189年由塔波扎杰的弟子都松钦巴创造，是噶玛噶举派（黑帽系）的主寺，也是藏传佛教最有影响的活佛转世制度的发源地，在国内外有较大影响。

43. A stele of the Tsurpu Monastery and the main hall.
    楚布寺石碑与大殿建筑。
44. The Mountain-girt Tsurpu Monastery.
    位于山谷中的楚布寺。
45. Scriptures preserved in the Tsurpu Monastery.
    寺藏经书。
46. A Buddhist statue of Esoteric Buddhism enshrined
    in the Tsurpu Monastery.
    寺内供奉的密宗佛像。
47. Details of a mural in the Tsurpu Monastery.
    寺内壁画局部。

	43	45	46
44			47

The Tashilhunpo Monastery 扎什伦布寺

Founded in 1447 by the First Dalai Lama, Gedun Truppa, in the city of Xigaze, Tibet, the Tashilhunpo Monastery has been the permanent residence of the successive Panchen Lamas. It is the largest monastery of the Gelug Sect in Posterior Tibet, as well as one of the six great monasteries of the Gelug Sect of Tibetan Buddhism. Tashilhunpo means "auspicious monastery of Mount Sumeru." The magnificent buildings of the monastery occupy an area of over 300,000 sq m. Among its innumerable treasures and relics, the most famous ones include a 26.7-m-high gilded bronze statue of Maitreya, the Buddha of the Future, built by the Ninth Panchen Lama with more than 6,700 *liang* (335 kg) of gold and over 115,000 kg of red copper, and inlaid with innumerable diamonds and other gems; a silver stupa—the Drashi Namgyal—that holds the remains of the fifth to the ninth Panchen Lamas, constructed at a huge cost; and a gold stupa—the Sersum Namgyal—built for the 10th Panchen Lama using 614 kg of gold, 275 kg of silver, and more than 10,000 precious stones and gems, at a cost of upwards of 67 million yuan. These magnificent and extravagantly decorated halls and stupas are the most grandiose and valuable examples of the religious art preserved in the monasteries of Tibetan Buddhism. Every year in mid-May by the Tibetan calendar, activities are held for three days to display the huge silk images of Tathagata— the Buddhas of the past, present and future. At this time the Tashilhunpo Monastery becomes the center of pilgrimage for both clerical and secular people of Tibetan Buddhism. On December 8,1995, a grand enthronement ceremony was held here for the 11th Panchen Lama, after he was chosen by drawing lots from the gold urn.

位于西藏日喀则市内，为第一世达赖根敦珠巴于1447年创建，后为历世班禅驻锡地，是西藏格鲁派在后藏地区最大的寺庙，也是藏传佛教格鲁派六大寺庙之一。"扎什伦布"藏语意为"吉祥须弥"。该寺建筑雄伟壮观、金碧辉煌，总面积约30多万平方米，藏有珍贵文物难以计数。最著名的有：九世班禅用紫铜23万多斤、黄金6700多两以及大量各种珍珠宝石修造的高26.7米的鎏金铜佛——强巴佛像；耗巨资为五至九世班禅遗骨合藏而修建的银质灵塔——扎什南捷；动用黄金614公斤、白银275公斤及各种珠宝7万余颗，共耗资6700多万元为第十世班禅修建的金质灵塔——释颂南捷等等。这些金碧辉煌，雄伟壮观的佛塔祀殿，都是该寺乃至藏传佛教各寺庙宗教艺术宝库中最宏伟、最珍贵、最有价值、最有代表性的文物珍品。藏历每年5月中旬，该寺将连续3天举行盛大的展佛活动，展示过去、现在、未来三世如来佛丝织巨幅佛像，届时扎什伦布寺成为广大藏传佛教僧俗群众最向往的朝圣中心。1995年12月8日，经金瓶掣签认定的第十一世班禅在此举行了隆重的坐床仪式。

48. The Drashi Namgyal Stupa, which holds the
    remains of the fifth to the ninth Panchen Lamas, was
    completed in 1989.
    1989 年竣工的五至九世班禅灵塔祀殿——扎什南捷。
49. A panoramic view of the Tashilhunpo Monastery.
    扎什伦布寺全景。

50. A solemn Buddhist service being held in the Tashilhunpo Monastery.

寺内正在举行隆重的佛事活动。

51. The gateway to the Drashi Namgyal Stupa Hall. (Photo by Wang Chunshu)

扎什南捷殿殿门。（王春树 摄）

52. This 26.7-m-high gilded bronze statue of Maitreya is the largest of its kind in the world. (Photo by Wang Chunshu)

高26.7米被称为世界上最大的强巴佛像。（王春树 慑）

53. A ceiling design in the Drashi Namgyal Stupa Hall.
(Photo by Wang Chunshu)
扎什南捷殿藻井。(王春树 摄)

54. The splendid gold stupa of the 10th Panchen Lama.
金碧辉煌的第十世班禅灵塔。

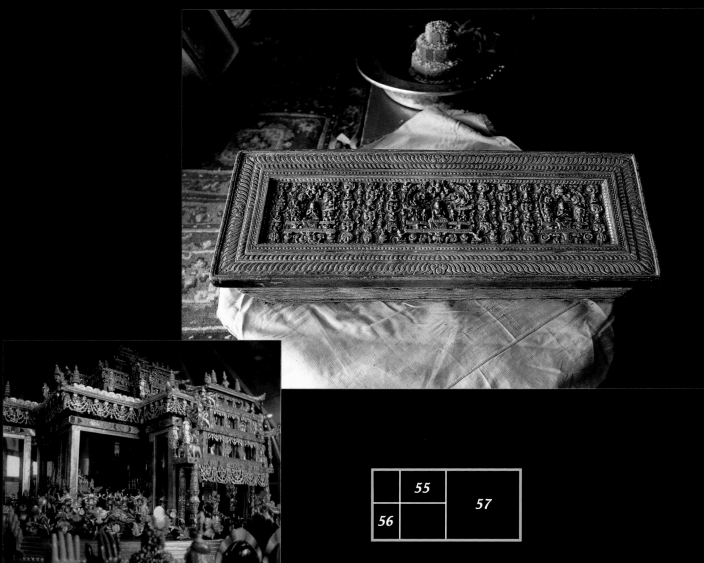

	55	
56		57

55. Scriptures preserved in the Tashilhunpo Monastery.
   (Photo by Wang Chunshu)
   寺内珍藏的经书.（王春树 摄）
56. The Hall of the Esoteric Mandala in the Tashilhunpo Monastery.
   寺内密宗坛城殿。
   The Buddha image displaying ceremony at the Tashilhunpo
57. Monastery.
   扎什伦布寺展佛。

The Sakya Monastery 萨迦寺

Located in the county town of Sakya (Sa'gya) in Xigaze Prefecture, the Sakya Monastery is the major monastery of the Sakya Sect of Tibetan Buddhism. As the political, religious and cultural center of Tibet in the 12th century, it has held an important and special position in the history of Tibetan Buddhism, and still does. The Sakya Monastery is composed of two parts: the Southern Monastery and the Northern Monastery. Construction of the northern one was initiated in 1073 by the founder of the Sakya Sect, Khon Konchok Gyalpo; the southern one was built in 1268 by the fifth patriarch of the Sakya Sect, Pagsba, with the human and material resources of 130,000 households in Tibet. Occupying an area of 45,000 sq m, the Southern Monastery looks like an ancient castle, surrounded by a moat and double walls. There is a tower at each corner of the square walls, with a watchtower in the middle. The monastery was constructed completely for defense, a unique work in Tibetan architectural history. Among the 40 wooden pillars in the main assembly hall of the Southern Monastery, four are made of cypress, all about 1.3 m in diameter and each with a beautiful and mystical story behind it. In the scripture repository is preserved a vast quantity of scriptures, among which the most famous and precious are the Tripitaka written in gold, silver and vermilion ink, and pattra-or palm-leaf scriptures written in Tibetan, Mongolian and Sanskrit. In addition to religion, these precious ancient scriptures and records also cover astronomy, the almanac, medicine, history, biography, philosophy, music, grammar and rhetoric. Various kinds of precious porcelain articles bestowed on the monastery by Ming and Qing emperors are also preserved there. With its high reputation, rich cultural relics, precious porcelains, voluminous scriptures, beautiful murals, elaborate woodcarvings, and numerous statues, the Sakya Monastery has been acclaimed as China's cultural treasure house second only to Dunhuang in Gansu Province.

位于西藏日喀则地区萨迦县城,是藏传佛教萨迦派主寺。12世纪这里曾成为西藏政治、宗教、文化的中心,因而在藏传佛教历史乃至今天都有着重大影响和特殊地位。该寺分南寺、北寺,北寺于1073年由萨迦派创始人昆·衮却杰波创建,南寺为著名的萨迦派第五祖师八思巴于公元1268年,集西藏13万户之人力物力修建。南寺占地约4.5万平方米,为一座城堡式建筑,四周有护城河和两重城墙,四角有角楼,四方城墙中有碉楼,形同古代的城池。这是一座完全以城防为目的而建的寺院,是西藏建筑艺术史上的一个突出范例。南寺大经堂内40多根原木立柱中,最有名的是4根直径约1.3米左右柏树立柱,它们各有着不同神奇的故事与美丽的传说。寺内闻名于世的经书墙,藏有各类经书万卷,其中最著名、最珍贵的是用金汁、银汁、朱砂等书写的大藏经,以及用藏文、蒙文和梵文刻写的贝叶经,这些珍贵的典籍、文物除宗教内容外,还涉及天文历算、医学、历史、人物传记、哲学、音乐、文法修辞等诸多方面。此外,元明两代朝廷赐给寺院的各种瓷器等,也是该寺特有的珍藏宝物。萨迦寺由于声誉之高,文物之丰,瓷器之珍,经书之浩,壁画之丽,木刻之精,造像之众,而被称为中国的第二个敦煌文化宝库。

58. The southern part of the Sakya Monastery by the Tromchu River.
萨迦寺（南寺）主殿。

59. The main hall of the southern part of the Sakya Monastery.
位于仲曲河畔的萨迦寺（南寺）

58

59

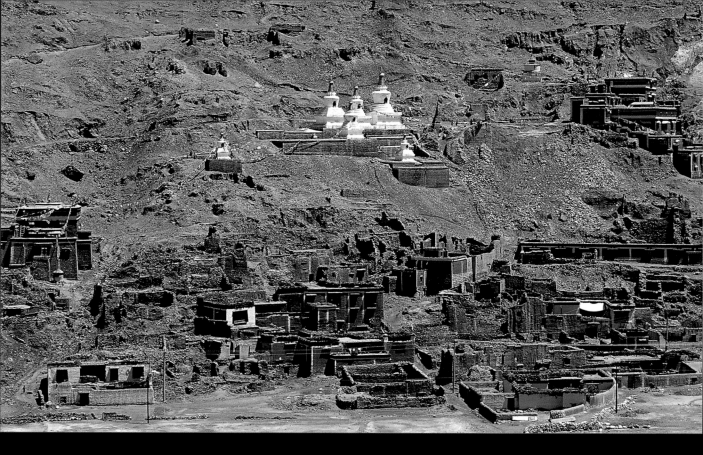

60. The ruins of the northern part of the Sakya Monastery.
    萨迦北寺遗迹。
61. The main assembly hall, supported by 40 wooden pillars,
    in the Sakya Monastery.
    有 40 根原木立柱的萨迦寺大经堂。

60	
	61

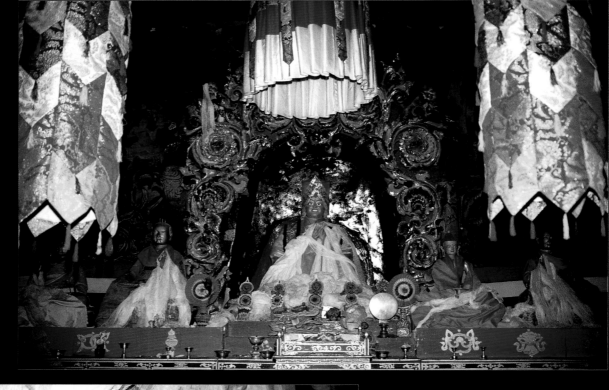

Monastery.
寺内供奉的佛像。

63. Thousands of ancient scriptures are preserved
in the monastery's scripture repository.
内藏万卷古老经典的经书墙（局部）。

64. Tripitaka written in silver ink.
用银汁书写的大藏经。

65. The famous mural in the Sakya Monastery.
著名的萨迦寺壁画。

The Shalu Monastery 夏鲁寺

Located 20 km southeast of Xigaze City, Tibet, the Shalu Monastery was established in the mid-11th century, and reached its present size after three expansions during the Yuan Dynasty. Its three-story main building is mostly in the Tibetan architectural style, but its glazed-tile roof is in the Han-Chinese style—a good example of the combined Han-Tibetan architectural styles. The Shalu Monastery is most famous for its murals. Covering mostly the Exoteric and Esoteric teachings of Buddhism, they are the quintessence of Tibetan Buddhist murals produced in the Yuan Dynasty (1271-1368), and had a strong impact on Tibetan mural art in the late Yuan, Ming (1368-1644) and Qing (1644-1911) dynasties. As a milestone in Tibetan artistic development during the Yuan and Ming dynasties, these murals are essential for the study of Tibetan art history during that period, and the artistic exchanges between Tibet and the Central Plains as well as foreign countries such as Nepal and India. Shalu means "new tender leaves" in Tibetan. The monastery was so named because its site was chosen in spring, when the surrounding trees were covered with tender leaves.

位于日喀则市东南约20公里处，建于11世纪中叶，经元代三次维修扩建形成今日的规模。该寺主体建筑为三层，墙体和布局为藏式建筑，屋顶为汉式琉璃瓦，是一座藏汉合璧建筑寺庙。该寺最著名的寺藏当属壁画，系元代藏传佛教壁画的典范，内容主要为显宗和密宗，它对元末明清西藏壁画艺术产生了重大影响，对研究元明两代西藏艺术史及该时期西藏艺术与中原，以及尼泊尔、印度等地间的相互交流有着重要参考价值，是元明两代西藏艺术发展史上的里程碑。"夏鲁"藏语意为新生嫩叶，相传当年建寺选址时，这里恰是植物嫩叶长满枝头之时，故取名"夏鲁"。

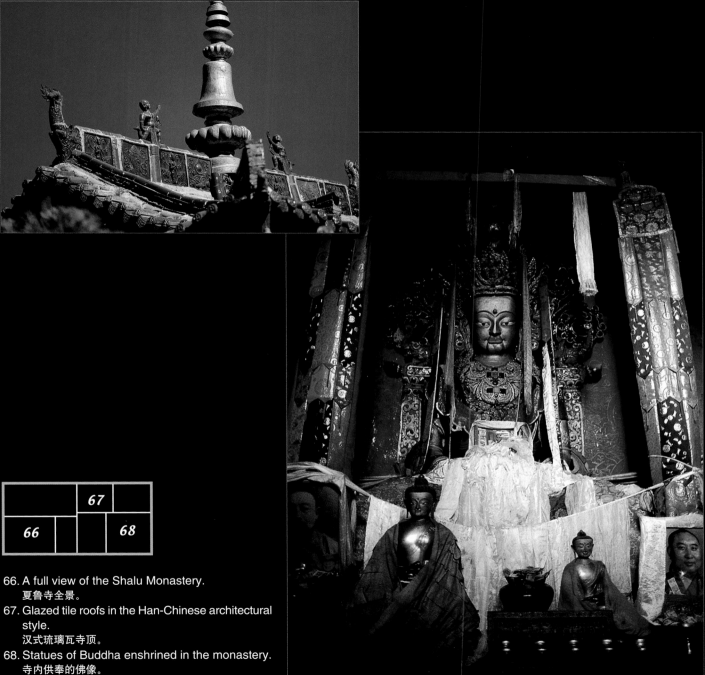

	67	
66		68

66. A full view of the Shalu Monastery.
夏鲁寺全景。
67. Glazed tile roofs in the Han-Chinese architectural style.
汉式琉璃瓦寺顶。
68. Statues of Buddha enshrined in the monastery.
寺内供奉的佛像。

Located at the foot of Mount Dzongri in Gyangze (Gyantse) County, Xigaze Prefecture, the two-story Tibetan-styled Pelkor Chode Monastery consists of temples, the multi-door white pagoda, and a Dratsang, or college. With its construction planned jointly by the religious king of Gyantse and the First Panchen Lama during the Ming Dynasty, the monastery was completed in 1425, after seven years. Ten years later, the Gyantse Kumbum Pagoda was erected next to the flat-roofed monastery. The nine-story white pagoda has four sides with eight corners, 108 doors, and 77 Buddha-halls, niches, and assembly halls. It is estimated that as many as 100,000 Buddhist statues are preserved in the pagoda, so it is also known as the "100,000-Buddha-Statue Pagoda." The monastery is typical of the temple-pagoda architectural style of Posterior Tibet during the period between the 13th and the 15th centuries. It is also the only completely preserved monastery combining architecture, painting and sculpture into one –a veritable museum of religious art. The Pelkor Chode Monastery is also unique in that every school of Tibetan Buddhism has its hall, and all schools exist side by side peacefully, in the same monastery.

位于西藏日喀则地区江孜县宗山脚下，由寺院、吉祥多门白塔，以及扎仓等组成。该寺始建于明代，为 2 层平顶藏式建筑，由江孜法王和一世班禅策划，历时7年于1425年建成。随后又历时10年于1436年在寺旁建成吉祥多门白塔。吉祥多门白塔高 9 层，外形四面八角，设 108 个门，77 间佛殿、神龛和经堂。殿堂内藏有大量佛像，据说多达十万，故又称十万佛塔。该寺为 13 至 15 世纪后藏地区塔、寺相互辉映的典型建筑，也是目前中国唯一一座集建筑、绘画和雕塑艺术于一身，至今保存完整的寺庙，堪称具有纪念碑性质的宗教艺术博物馆。该寺的独特之处还在于：藏传佛教各教派和平共存于一寺，每个教派在此寺内都拥有自己的殿堂。

69. Painted patterns on the Pelkor Chode Pagoda.
白居塔建筑上绘饰的图案。

70. Butter sculpture sacrifices before the shrine.
佛堂前酥油花供品。

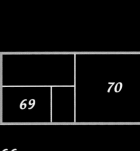

	70
69	

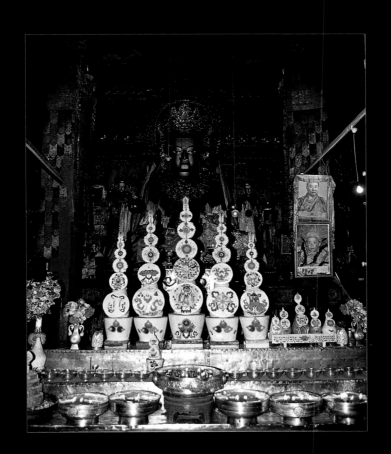

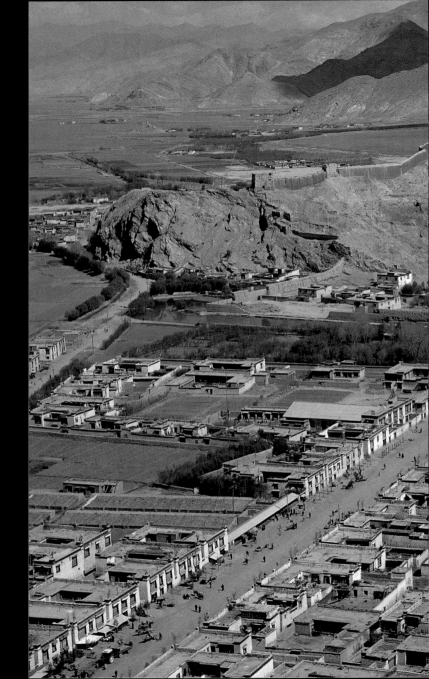

71

71. The Pelkor Chode Monastery in the ancient town
of Gyantse.
位于江孜古城内的白居寺。

72. Buddhist statues in the monastery.
寺内佛像雕塑。
73. The Pelkor Chode Pagoda is also known as the
"100,000-Buddha-Statue Pagoda."
有十万佛塔之称的白居塔。

| 72 | 73 |

The Rongpo Monastery 绒布寺

Situated at the foot of Mount Qomolangma, 5,300 m above sea level in Tingri County, Xigaze Prefecture, the Rongpo Monastery was built in the 16th century. Small as it is, the monastery is famous as a monastery on the highest elevation in the world. It is now a destination for both explorers and tourists. The monastery also serves as the base camp site for the Chinese National Mountaineering Team.

位于西藏日喀则地区定日县境内的珠穆朗玛峰脚下海拔5300米处，始建于16世纪。该寺虽小，却因其海拔最高而名扬海内外。该寺现为珠峰探险、考察、旅游的景点，又是中国登山队大本营所在地。

74. The Rongpo Monastery is located at the highest altitude in the world.
世界上海拔最高的寺庙绒布寺。

75. A monk in the Rongpo Monastery.
绒布寺修行的僧人。

76. Building and murals in the Rongpo Monastery.
寺内建筑及壁画。

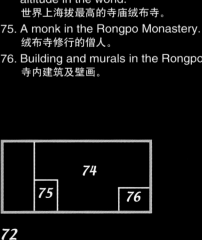

	74	
75		76

The Samye Monastery 桑耶寺

In Tibetan the Samye Monastery means "ever-auspicious heaven-protected great monastery." Situated on the northern bank of the Yarlungzangbo River in Zhanang County, Shannan Prefecture, Tibet, the Samye Monastery was constructed in the mid-eighth century by a Tibetan king, Trisong Detsen, in imitation of Indian temples. As it was the first Buddhist monastery built in the Tubo Kingdom period that integrated the Triratna or three treasures—the Buddha, dharma (law) and Sangha (community of believers)—into one, the monastery was very important and influential in Tibetan Buddhist history. With a blending of Tibetan, Han-Chinese and Indian architectural styles, its main hall, a symbol of Mount Sumeru, is a three-story building: The first story is in the traditional Tibetan style; the middle one in the Han-Chinese style, and the top one in the Indian style. On each side of the entrance to the main hall, there is a stone lion which is said to date back more than 1,000 years to the Tubo Kingdom period. An ancient bell hanging over the entrance is reportedly a Tang Dynasty relic—a treasure of the monastery that still clearly retains ancient inscriptions. There is a pagoda at each corner of the monastery: The green pagoda in the northeast represents Mahayana Buddha; the white one in the southeast stands for Shravaka, or the personal disciples of the Buddha; the red one in the southwest refers to Mahayana Bodhisattva; while the black one in the northwest represents Pratyekabuddha, the "Lonely Buddha." Enclosed in the high walls are temples of the Sakya, Nyingma, and Gelug sects of Tibetan Buddhism, separated by walls and each with its own tenets and disciples.

位于西藏山南地区扎囊县境内雅鲁藏布江北岸，藏文意为"吉祥永固天成桑耶大迦蓝"。该寺建于8世纪中叶，由藏王赤松德赞主持仿印度古寺而建。寺院融藏、汉、印建筑风格于一体，是吐蕃时期西藏第一座佛法僧三宝齐全的佛教寺院，因此该寺在藏传佛教历史上有着极其重要的地位和影响。寺内大殿象征须弥山，底层为藏式，中层为汉式，顶层为印度风格，故又称"三样式"。正殿大门两侧各有一尊石狮，相传为吐蕃时期之物，门廊上悬挂一口古钟，钟上铭文犹存，据说为唐代遗物，是该寺一宝。大殿四角各有一塔，东北角为绿色塔，代表大乘佛；东南角为白色塔，代表小乘声闻；西南角为红色塔，代表大乘菩萨；西北角为黑色塔，代表小乘独觉。该寺有高墙相围，历史上藏传佛教萨迦、宁玛、格鲁诸派同刹相处、各派筑墙为界，传法授徒。因此该寺既是萨迦道场，但又为各教派共同供奉。

77. The main hall of the Samye Monastery.
寺庙主殿建筑。
78. A stele in front of the Samye Monastery recording its history.
矗立在寺前记录寺庙简史的石碑。
79. The bell hanging over the main gate of the Samye Monastery is said to date from the Tang Dynasty (618-907).
悬挂在寺庙正门上方的古钟相传为唐代遗物。

80. A distant view of the Samye Monastery.
桑耶寺远眺。

81. The black pagoda in the northwest corner of the Samye Monastery.
位于该寺西北角的黑色佛塔。

82. Gilded Buddha statue enshrined in the Samye Monastery.
寺内供奉的鎏金佛像。

83. A statue of a 1,000-handed and 1,000-eyed Buddha.
寺内工艺精湛的千手千眼佛像。

84. One of the superb murals in the Samye Monastery.
著名的桑耶寺壁画。

81	82	84
	83	

The Trandruk Monastery is located in Zetang, capital of Shannan Prefecture. Dating back 1,300 years to the Tubo Kingdom period, the monastery used to be the winter palace of Songtsen Gampo and his wife Princess Wencheng. Its complete name is the "Trandruk Champa Ever-Stable Temple." Trandruk in Tibetan means "eagle and dragon." A story goes that there used to be an evil dragon in the area before the monastery was established. Songtsen Gampo turned into an eagle and subdued the dragon before the monastery could be built. The monastery was renovated and expanded under the supervision of Chief Minister Tagesidu Changchub Gyaltsen of the Pamotrupa regime in the 12th century, and many more repairs were also made later. Among its many treasures the most famous is an image of the goddess Tara. This 2-m-by-1.2-m picture is formed with over 2,900 pearls, in addition to diamonds, rubies, sapphires, turquoises and pieces of coral.

位于西藏山南地区首府泽当镇，为吐蕃时期建筑，距今有1300多年历史。相传该寺为藏王松赞干布和文成公主的冬宫，又称"昌珠强巴永固庙"。藏语"昌"为鹰、鹞之意，"珠"意为龙。传说建寺前此地有一恶龙，被松赞干布化为大鹏降伏后才得以建寺，故名曰"昌珠"。帕木竹巴王朝时期的大司徒降曲坚赞对该寺做过大规模扩建和改建，后又多次修缮。该寺藏有诸多珍宝，其中最著名的为一幅用珍珠缀成的度母像，长2米，宽1.2米，共耗珍珠2900多颗，另有钻石和红、蓝、紫色宝石，绿松石与珊瑚等各种珠宝，被称为该寺无价的镇寺之宝。

85. The ancient Trandruk Monastery.
昌珠古寺。

86. The most prized treasure of the Trandruk Monastery—an image of Tara formed with pearls.
镇寺之宝——珍珠度母像。

The Yumbulagang 雍布拉康

Situated on a hill on the east bank of the Yalong River in Nedong County, Shannan, the Yumbulagang was the first palace built in Tibet. It was later turned into a monastery. Assumedly built in the 2nd century BC, the fortress-like palace is rather small in size, but it has been regarded as holy by eminent Buddhist monks, and is now a well-known tourist attraction.

位于西藏山南乃东县雅砻河东岸一座小山上，是西藏历史上第一座宫殿。相传始建于公元前2世纪，后成为藏传佛教寺庙。该寺外形如碉堡，规模不大，但一向为佛教高僧的修行圣地，如今成为山南乃至西藏著名的旅游景点。

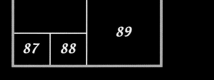

87.88. The Yumbulagang is the oldest palace in Tibet.
西藏历史上的第一座宫殿雍布拉康。

89. Buddhist statue enshrined in the Yumbulagang.
宫内供奉的佛像。

The Toling Monastery 托林寺

Located in the county town of Zanda in Ngari Prefecture, the Toling Monastery was founded by Yeshe Od, the leading lama of the Guge Kingdom in the 11th century for the great translator Rinchen Sangpo to translate and teach the scriptures. Toling in Tibetan means "ever flying in the sky," and the full name of the monastery is the "Golden Monastery of Toling." It was the first Tibetan Buddhist monastery in the Ngari area, where the renowned Indian Buddhist master Atisha once lived for three years when he came to preach in Tibet. It is the most representative monastery and also the most widely known historical site in the Ngari area, besides the ruins of the Guge Kingdom.

位于西藏阿里地区扎达县城，11世纪由阿里古格王国僧王益西沃为大译师仁钦桑布译经传道而建，全名"托林金殿"。"托林"，意为"空中飞翔不坠落"，这是阿里地区第一座藏传佛教寺院。印度著名佛教大师阿底峡入藏传教时曾在此居住3年，因而该寺也是阿里地区除古格王国遗址外最有影响和最有代表性的寺庙。

90. The Toling Monastery is located in a desert.
被荒漠包围的托林寺。
91. The main assembly hall of the Toling Monastery.
寺庙大经堂。

92. Ancient murals in the Toling Monastery.
寺内古老的壁画。

93. Ritual horns preserved in the monastery.
寺藏珍稀兽角。

94. An age-old prayer wheel.
寺内古老的转经桶。

		93
92		94

The Champa Ling 强巴林寺

The Champa Ling stands on the fourth terrace in the town of Qamdo, capital of Qamdo Prefecture in eastern Tibet, occupying an area of over 20 ha. Established in 1437 by Sherab Sangpo, a disciple of Tsongkhapa, the monastery is consecrated to Maitreya, the Buddha of the Future, or Champa in Tibetan, hence its name. In 1719, during the Qing Dynasty, Emperor Kangxi conferred the honorific title Preacher of Yellow Dharma Erdeni Hutuktu on Phapalha. Jigme Tanpel Gyatso. Later Qing emperors Qianlong, Xianfeng, Tongzhi and Guangxu also conferred honorific titles on the seventh, eighth and ninth Phapalhas. The present vice-chairman of the National Committee of the Chinese People's Political Consultative Conference (CPPCC), Phapalha. Gelek Namgyel, is the 11th reincarnation of Phapalha.

位于西藏东部昌都地区首府昌都镇第4阶台地上，占地 20 多公顷。该寺由宗喀巴弟子西尧桑布于公元1437年建立，寺庙主佛为强巴佛（弥勒佛），故取名为强巴林寺。公元1719年，康熙帝敕封帕巴拉·晋美丹贝嘉措"讲衍黄法额尔德尼呼图克图"名号，之后第七、八、九世帕巴拉又受乾隆、咸丰、同治、光绪等历代皇帝册封。现任全国政协副主席的帕巴拉·格列朗杰为该寺第十一世帕巴拉活佛。

95. The Champa Ling is the largest Tibetan Buddhist monastery in eastern Tibet.
强巴林寺 —— 藏东最大的藏传佛教寺庙。

96. Prayer wheels for use by pilgrims.
环绕在寺周围，供朝佛人用的传经桶。

97. A Buddhist service being performed in the Champa Ling.
寺庙内正在举行的佛事活动。

	96	
95		97

The Shabten Monastery 孝登寺

The Shabten Monastery is located in Nagqu Town, capital of Nagqu Prefecture, a sparsely-populated pastoral region of Tibet. Though small in size, it is the largest monastery of Tibetan Buddhism in northern Tibet.

位于西藏那曲地区首府那曲镇，由于那曲地区是西藏的牧区，人口较少，虽然该寺规模不大，却是藏北地区最大的藏传佛教寺庙。

98. The Shabten Monastery is located on the Changtang grassland.
    位于羌塘草原上的孝登寺。
99. White pagodas by the monastery.
    寺外白塔。
100. A mural in the Shabten Monastery.
    孝登寺壁画。

98		100
	99	

101. Buddhist statues enshrined in the Shabten Monastery.
寺内供奉的佛像。

102. Monks performing a Buddhist ceremony in the monastery.
举行佛事活动的寺庙僧人。

101

102

The Lama Ling 喇嘛林寺

Located in Nyingchi County, Tibet, the Lama Ling was founded in 1925 by the Nyingma Sect, or the Red Sect, of Tibetan Buddhism. Unique in architectural style, it is the largest monastery of Tibetan Buddhism in the Nyingchi area.

位于西藏林芝县境内，始建于1925年，为宁玛派红教寺庙。寺院建筑外形独特，是林芝地区规模最大的藏传佛教寺庙。

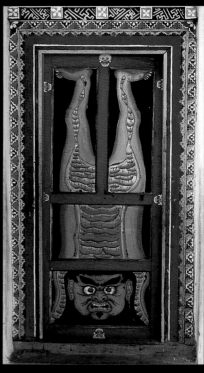

103. Buddhist statue enshrined in the Lama Ling.
寺内供奉的佛像。
104. A mural in the Lama Ling.
寺内壁画。
105. A view of the Lama Ling.
喇嘛林寺外景。

The Kumbum Monastery 塔尔寺

Situated southwest of Lusha'er Town in Huangzhong County, Qinghai Province, this 40-plus-ha monastery is the largest Tibetan Buddhist monastery in the province and one of the six great monasteries of the Gelug Sect, or Yellow Hat Sect, of Tibetan Buddhism in China. Sprawling on a hill, the monastery consists of halls of different sizes with golden-tiled roofs — the prayer hall, the main assembly hall, the Hall of Bodhisattva Manjusri, the eight pagodas of the Buddha, and the College of the Wheel of Time. The first building erected here was a lotus-shaped pagoda, built in 1379 by the mother of Tsongkhapa in the very place where he was born. Over a period of 17 years starting from 1560, other buildings were added, and the monastery got the name Kumbum Jampa Ling, meaning "a monastery of Maitreya with 100,000 lions roaring before the statue of the Buddha." The monastery's main building is a large hall roofed with golden tiles. This is a three-story building in combined Han and Tibetan architectural styles. Housed in the hall is Tsongkhapa's stupa, 11 m high and with a silver base gold-plated and inlaid with pearls and gems. The main assembly hall, with 108 square columns, is a typical Tibetan flat-roofed structure. The Kumbum Monastery is especially famous for its "three bests": butter sculptures, murals and embossed embroideries, which are treasures of Tibetan Buddhist art and widely acclaimed both within and outside China.

位于青海省湟中县鲁沙尔镇西南，占地 40 多公顷，是青海省最大的藏传佛教寺庙，也是藏传佛教格鲁派六大寺庙之一。整个寺院依山势起伏而建，由大小金瓦殿、祈祷殿、大经堂、文殊菩萨殿、如来八塔、时轮经院等组成。该寺址为格鲁派创始人宗喀巴大师的诞生地。1379年宗喀巴的母亲在其降生的地方建起一座莲花宝塔，并修一瓦屋以覆塔身，此处便是塔尔寺最早的建筑。1560年及其后的17年间，这里陆续修建了供僧人习经坐禅的禅堂和佛、法、僧俱全的弥勒佛殿，藏语合称"贡本贤巴林"，意为"十万狮子吼佛像的弥勒寺"，汉语称"塔尔寺"。该寺三层大金殿为全寺中心，是一座具有藏汉合璧式的金顶大殿，内供宗喀巴灵塔，高11米，底座为纯银制作，镀以黄金，上镶各种珠宝。有108根四楞明柱的大经堂，是典型的藏式平顶式结构。塔尔寺的酥油花、壁画和堆绣合称为寺中"三绝"，也是藏传佛教艺术宝库中的奇葩，称誉中外。

106. The main assembly hall of the Kumbum Monastery. (Photo by Zhai Dongfeng)
塔尔寺大经堂。（翟东风 摄）

107. Butter sculpture, one of the "three bests" of the Kumbum Monastery.
(Photo by Zhai Dongfeng)
"三绝"之一酥油花。（翟东风 摄）

108. Details of a butter sculpture "Princess Wencheng Entering Tibet."
塔尔寺著名的酥油花供品──文成公主进藏图（局部）。

109. Embossed embroidery, one of the "three bests" of the Kumbum Monastery, on display in a courtyard of the monastery.
(Photo by Zhai Dongfeng)
塔尔寺下花院正在展示寺中"三绝"之一堆绣。（翟东风 摄）

110	**111**
	112

110. A panoramic view of the Kumbum
Monastery. (Photo by Zhai Dongfeng)
塔尔寺全景。（翟东风 摄）

111. The stupa of Tsongkhapa, founder of
the Gelug Sect.
(Photo by Zhai Dongfeng)
宗喀巴大师灵塔。（翟东风 摄）

112. A Great Prayer Meeting is held twice a
year in the Kumbum Monastery.
塔尔寺正月法会。（翟东风 摄）

The Kyegu Monastery 结古寺

The Kyegu Monastery is located in Kyegu Town, capital of the Yushu Tibetan Autonomous Prefecture in Qinghai Province. Built against a mountain, this majestic monastery belongs to the Sakya Sect of Tibetan Buddhism. It was established by the noted Sakya monk Dangchenwa Jamyang Sherab Gyaltsen, who came to preach here in 1398. The Ninth Panchen Erdeni Chokyi Nyima passed away in the monastery on his way back to Tibet from the hinterland on December 1, 1937 by the Tibetan calendar.

　　位于青海省玉树藏族自治州州府所在地结古镇，藏语全称"结古顿珠林"。该寺依山而建，气势宏伟，为藏传佛教萨迦派寺院。1398年，萨迦派名僧当钦哇·嘉昂喜绕坚赞来此传教创建此寺。1937年藏历12月1日，第九世班禅大师洛桑·确吉尼玛在由内地返藏途中于该寺圆寂。

113. A corner of the Kyegu Monastery.
寺内一角。
114. Halls and monks' quarters in the Kyegu Monastery.
殿堂僧舍错落有致的结古寺。

Monastery was established in 1709 by the first Jamyang reincarnated lama, Ngawang Tsondre. It is the largest Tibetan Buddhist monastery in Gansu Province and also one of the six major monasteries of the Gelug Sect of Tibetan Buddhism. There are six Dratsang or monastic colleges: the College of the Exoteric Buddhism; the Upper and Lower Tantric colleges of Esoteric Buddhism; the College of the Happy Thunderbolt, where religious ceremonies are studied; the College of the Wheel of Time, where astronomy, geography, the Tibetan calendar and almanacs, and mathematics are studied; and the medical and pharmaceutical college, where traditional Tibetan medicine is studied. The Labrang Monastery has cultivated a crop of scholars and Buddhist masters. Contributing greatly to the development of Tibetan Buddhism, the monastery has a strong influence on other monasteries run by different sects.

由第一世嘉木样活佛阿旺宗哲于1709年创建，为甘肃最大的藏传佛教寺庙，也是藏传佛教格鲁派六大寺庙之一。寺内设有六大扎仓（学院）：修习显宗的闻思学院；修习密宗的上、下续部学院；修法事的喜金刚学院；学习天文地理和数学的时轮学院，每年编制藏族年历和黄历；医药学院，学习藏医等。由于该寺注重学修，寺规严格，因而高僧、学者层出不穷，在藏传佛教的发展史上，以及各教派寺庙中都具有重要地位和影响。

115. The Labrang Monastery is famous among Tibetan Buddhist monasteries as the highest institute of Lamaist learning. (Photo by Dong Ruicheng)
拉卜楞寺在藏传佛教寺庙中地位显赫，并堪称喇嘛教中的最高学府。（董瑞成 摄）

116. The Pagoda of the Living Buddha Gungthang Tsang. (Photo by Dong Ruicheng)
贡唐仓活佛宝塔。（董瑞成 摄）

115	116

117. The Great Prayer Meetings are held twice every year from January 4 to 17 and from June 29 to July 15 by the lunar calendar in the Labrang Monastery. On these occasions, activities include Sunning the Buddha—displaying a large Thangka depicting the historical Buddha Sakyamuni — Buddhist dances, and debates and arguments. The photo shows a Buddhist dance. (Photo by Yuan Xuejun)

拉卜楞寺每年农历正月初四至十七日、六月廿九至七月十五日，举办两次大法会。活动有晒大佛、法舞、辩经等。图为大法会上的法舞。（袁学军 摄）

118. Monks at a Great Prayer Meeting. (Photo by Yuan Xuejun)

大法会上的众僧们。（袁学军 摄）

117

118

The Chamchen Chokhor Monastery 长春科尔寺

Located in Litang County in the Tibetan Autonomous Prefecture of Garze in Sichuan Province, this monastery covers an area of 34 ha. It was founded by the Third Dalai Lama, Sonam Gyatro, in 1580, during the Ming Dynasty. A profusion of precious relics are housed in the monastery. With a high reputation in the Tibetan-inhabited areas, the Chamchen Chokhor Monastery is an important center of the Gelug Sect, and also the largest Tibetan Buddhist monastery in Sichuan Province.

位于四川省甘孜藏族自治州理塘县境内，占地约34公顷，系三世达赖索南嘉措于明万历八年（公元1580年）创建，距今已有400多年历史。寺内藏有珍贵文物，历史上曾传有"上有拉萨三大寺，下有安多塔尔寺，中有理塘长春寺"之说，有很高声誉，是重要的格鲁派黄教寺院，也是四川省规模最大的藏传佛教寺院。

119. A grand inauguration
cere-mony was held after
the main hall was rebuilt.
(Photo by Wang Dajun)
大殿重建后的开光仪典。
（王达军 摄）

120. An eight-m-high gilded
Budd-hist statue in the
main assembly hall.
(Photo by Wang Dajun)
大经堂内高约 8 米的镏金佛像。
（王达军 摄）

119

120

121	123
122	

121. Chanting sutras in the main assembly hall.
(Photo by Wang Dajun)
在大经堂内诵经。（王达军 摄）
122. Monks making buttered tea at the Chamchen Chokhor Monastery. (Photo by Wang Dajun)
长青春科尔寺内的喇嘛们正在打酥油茶。（王达军 摄）
123. A painted statue of a dharma guardian.
(Photo by Wang Dajun)
彩塑护法神像。（王达军 摄）

The Ganden Songtsen Ling 噶丹·松赞林寺

The Ganden Songtsen Ling is situated in Shangri-La County (formerly named Zhongdian County) in the Tibetan Autonomous Prefecture of Deqen, in Yunnan Province. Also known as the Guihua Monastery, it was founded in 1659 and is the largest Tibetan Buddhist monastery in Yunnan. Built against a mountain, the monastery features a layout similar to that of the Potala Palace in Lhasa, except that it is surrounded by an oval wall. Centering on the main hall, there are 100 rooms for reincarnated lamas as well as for ordinary monks. The main hall, supported by 116 pillars, can accommodate up to a thousand worshippers at a time.

位于云南省迪庆藏族自治州香格里拉县（原中甸县）境内，又称归化寺，为云南省最大的藏传佛教寺院，始建于1659年。该寺仿布达拉宫布局，依山而建，外围建成椭圆形城垣。主殿周围散布有百间活佛静室及僧舍，形成气势宏大的藏式碉房建筑群。大殿由116根立柱支撑，可容上千人朝拜诵经。

124

124. The magnificent Ganden Songtsen Ling.
气势不凡的噶丹·松赞林寺。

125. A mural in the Ganden Songtsen Ling.
寺内壁画。

126. The abbot of the Ganden Songtsen Ling.
松赞林寺主持。

127. The magnificent main hall of the Ganden Songtsen Ling. (Photo by Lan Peijin)
雄伟的大殿。（兰佩瑾 摄）

Temples on Mount Wutai 五台山

Situated in Wutai County, Shanxi Province, Mount Wutai, with 43 temples, is the first of the four sacred mountains of Buddhism in China. The temples on Mount Wutai became related to Tibetan Buddhism in the Yuan Dynasty. In the early years of the Qing Dynasty (1644-1911), Emperor Shunzhi decreed that 10 of the temples on Mount Wutai be changed into Tibetan Buddhist temples. The Pusading Temple on Lingjiu Peak is the largest Tibetan Buddhist temple on Mount Wutai. It is said that the Sixth Dalai Lama, Tsangyang Gyatso, once lived in the Guanyin (Goddess of Mercy) Cave (also known as the Qixian Temple) in Qixian Valley. The small Buddhist chapel there is also very famous among Tibetans and Mongolians for being a place where the 13th Dalai Lama meditated.

位于山西省五台县境内，现存寺庙43处，为中国佛教四大佛山之首。五台山寺庙与藏传佛教结缘始于元代。清初，顺治皇帝将五台山10座寺庙改为藏传佛教寺庙。坐落在灵鹫山的菩萨顶，是该地最大的藏传佛教寺庙，而位于栖贤谷口的观音洞（又称栖贤寺），相传六世达赖喇嘛仓央嘉措曾在此住过；而寺中的音积小佛殿，是十三世达赖喇嘛的静坐处，因而该寺成为在蒙藏地区极有影响的藏传佛教寺庙。

128. A panoramic view of Taihuai Town, the center of the 43 Buddhist temples on Mount Wutai. Top right is the Pusading Temple. (Photo by Du Dianwen)

五台山台怀镇全景。右侧上部建筑为菩萨顶。（杜殿文　摄）

128

29. The Zhuoni edition of the *Kangyur* included in the Tripitaka preserved in the Shifangtang Temple on Mount Wutai. It is the oldest edition of this sutra extant in China. (Photo by Du Dianwen)

五台山十方堂内珍藏的大藏经《甘珠尔》卓尼版，为国内现存最古老的原版大藏经经卷。（杜殿文　摄）

30. The stupa of the 15th Changkya Reincarnated Lama in the Zhenhai Temple on Mount Wutai (Changkya, Dalai, Panchen, and Jetsun Dampa were the four Tibetan-Mongolian lama reincarnation systems of the Qing Dynasty.) (Photo by Du Dianwen)

镇海寺十五世章嘉活佛（清代与达赖、班禅、哲布尊丹巴并称为藏、蒙四大活佛系统）灵塔。（杜殿文　摄）

31. Monks making a pilgrimage to Beitaiding Peak on Mount Wutai. (Photo by Du Dianwen)

在五台山北台顶朝觐的僧人。（杜殿文　摄）

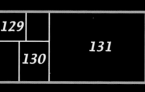

The Eight Outlying Temples Surrounding the Chengde Imperial Summer Resort

承德外八庙

The eight outer temples stand to the northeast of the Chengde Imperial Summer Resort in Hebei Province. From 1713 to 1780 during the Qing Dynasty, emperors Kangxi and Qianlong built 12 temples outside the Imperial Summer Resort, which were administered by eight institutions. Among these, the more famous and grander ones are the Temple of the Potaraka Doctrine, Puning Temple, Temple of Sumeru Happiness and Longevity, Pule Temple, Anyuan Temple and Puren Temple.

位于河北省承德避暑山庄的东北部。自1713年至1780年57年间，清廷康熙和乾隆在避暑山庄周围共建寺庙12座，分由8个机构管理，故称外八庙。其中规模气势较大并影响至今的主要有普陀宗乘之庙、普宁寺、须弥福寿之庙、普乐寺、安远庙及溥仁寺等。

The Temple of the Potaraka Doctrine

普陀宗乘之庙

The largest of these temples, the Temple of the Potaraka Doctrine has an area of 216,000 sq m. It was completed in 1770 for entertaining the princes and distinguished monks of minority ethnic groups who came to Chengde to celebrate Emperor Qianlong's 60th birthday and his mother's 80th birthday. A replica of Lhasa's Potala Palace, the temple is resplendent and magnificent, and has a collection of eight valuable Buddhist ritual implements, an enamel pagoda and a statue of Sakyamuni.

外八庙中规模最大的寺庙，该寺占地 21.6 万平方米，于 1770 年竣工，是为了接待前来为乾隆 60 岁寿辰、皇太后 80 岁寿辰祝寿的少数民族王公和高僧而建，外观与西藏布达拉宫极为相像，金碧辉煌，气势宏大，内供奉珐琅塔、法器八宝及佛祖释迦牟尼佛像，因而有小布达拉宫之称。

132. The Temple of the Potaraka Doctrine is a replica of Lhasa's Potala Palace.
(Photo by Lan Peijin)
外八庙中的普陀宗乘之庙，仿西藏布达拉宫建筑。
（兰佩瑾 摄）

133. The Five-Pagoda Gate in the temple, on which the five pagodas represent different schools of Lamaism.
(Photo by Lan Peijin)
庙中的五塔门，门上并立五座形式各异的喇嘛塔，分别代表喇嘛教各派。
（兰佩瑾 摄）

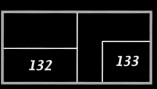

132 133

119

134

135

134. The red elevated platform is the major feature of the Temple of the Potaraka Doctrine. The photo shows the golden roof of its central hall. (Photo by Lan Peijin)

普陀宗乘之庙主体建筑是大红台。图为大红台中部的万法归一殿金顶。（兰佩瑾 摄）

135. The Temple of Sumeru Happiness and Longevity is also known as the Panchen Lama Temple. (Photo by Lan Peijin)

建于公元1780年的须弥福寿之庙，又称班禅庙。（兰佩瑾 摄）

The Temple of Sumeru Happiness and Longevity 须弥福寿之庙

On the occasion of the 70th birthday of Emperor Qianlong in 1780, the Sixth Panchen Lama came specially from Tibet to Chengde with a 2,000-strong entourage to celebrate the anniversary and pay homage to the emperor. To welcome the Sixth Panchen Lama and his party, Emperor Qianlong had a replica of Xigaze's Tashilhunpo Monastery built in Chengde—the Temple of the Sumeru Happiness and Longevity.

乾隆 70 岁寿辰时，六世班禅亲率 2000 多人专程自西藏赴承德祝贺朝觐，为接待六世班禅及其随行人员，乾隆皇帝特命仿西藏日喀则扎什伦布寺样式修建须弥福寿之庙，意为"富寿吉祥的须弥山"。

The Puning (Universal Peace) Temple　普宁寺

Copied from the Samye Monastery in Tibet, it displays both Han and Tibetan architectural styles. Built in 1755, it covers an area of 33,000 sq m. The temple features in its Mahayana Hall an exquisite wooden statue of the Goddess of Mercy, depicted with 1,000 arms and 1,000 eyes. Sculpted from 120 cu m of wood, it is the largest such statue in the world—22.8 m in height, 15 m in waist girth and weighing 110 tons.

占地3.3万平方米，始建于1755年，仿西藏桑耶寺建筑，属汉藏建筑风格。中心建筑为"大乘之阁"，并供奉一尊身高22.8米、腰粗15米，用120立方米木材建筑，重110吨的千手千眼观音菩萨佛像，为世界木雕佛像之最。

136. The images of Tara in the Mahavira (Great Hero) Hall are prized treasures among the murals in the Eight Outlying Temples of Chengde. (Photo by Du Dianwen)
大雄宝殿内的度母像，是外八庙诸寺壁画中的精品。（杜殿文　摄）

137. The Puning Temple. (Photo by Lan Peijin)
该寺的藏式建筑仿西藏桑耶寺的"曼陀罗"布局。（兰佩瑾　摄）

138. The Mahayana Hall in the Puning Temple, also known as the Sanyang Tower, is a replica of the Utse Hall of the Samye Monastery. (Photo by Du Dianwen)
寺内大乘之阁又名三阳楼，仿桑耶寺乌策大殿建造。（杜殿文　摄）

136	
	138
137	

The Wudangzhao Monastery 五当召

Located in Wudanggou Valley, northeast of Baotou City in the Inner Mongolia Autonomous Region, the Wudangzhao Monastery was founded in 1749 and underwent several large expansions later. In 1754, the monastery was given the name Guangjue Temple by the Board of Ethnic Affairs. The reincarnated lama of the monastery, Erdeni. Morgen Dongkorda Pandita, was one the eight resident Hutuktus in Beijing during the Qing Dynasty.

位于内蒙古自治区包头市东北五当沟内。创建于1749年，后几经扩建，公元1754年理藩院赐名"广觉寺"。该寺活佛号为"额尔德尼·莫日根·洞科达·班智达"，清代，曾是驻京八大呼图克图之一。

139. The Wudangzhao Monastery is located at the foot of Mount Yinshan. (Photo by Du Dianwen)
座落在阴山脚下的五当召。（杜殿文　摄）
140. The 10-m-high bronze statue of Tsongkhapa in the Namling Temple is the largest of its kind extant in Inner Mongolia. (Photo by Du Dianwen)
那木林独贡内的宗喀巴铜像高10米，是内蒙古现存最大的铜佛像。（杜殿文　摄）
141. The College of Buddhism was set up in the Wudangzhao Monastery by the government of the Inner Mongolia Autonomous Region. (Photo by Du Dianwen)
内蒙古自治区在五当召开办的佛教学校。（杜殿文　摄）
142. The annual Mani Buddhist ceremony being held at the Wudangzhao Monastery. (Photo by Du Dianwen)
庙内的喇嘛正在举办一年一度的嘛尼佛事活动。（杜殿文　摄）

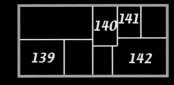

自治区
内蒙古
佛教学校

The Yonghegong Lamasery 雍和宫

Standing on Yonghegong Street in the Eastern District of Beijing, the Yonghegong Lamasery is the largest Tibetan Buddhist monastery in Beijing. It used to be the residence of Emperor Yongzheng before he took the throne. After his enthronement, it became an imperial palace for short stays outside the Forbidden City and was named the Yonghegong Palace in 1725. It was converted into a Tibetan Buddhist monastery of the Gelug Sect in 1744.

The 66,400-sq-m monastery is composed of the Yonghegong main hall, Yongyou Hall, Falun Hall and Wanfu Tower. The Wanfu Tower is also called the Great Buddha Tower, where a giant white sandalwood statue of Maitreya or the Buddha of the Future is enshrined. This is the largest single-trunk wooden sculpture in China. This statue, of world renown, is 26 m in height and eight m in diameter, with 8 m below the ground. It weighs 100 tons. With its rich collection of precious relics and treasures, the monastery attracts streams of pilgrims and tourists all year round. It is not only a sanctuary of Buddhism in China's capital but also a treasure house of the art and culture of the Han, Manchu, Mongolian and Tibetan ethnic groups.

坐落于北京市东城区雍和宫大街，是北京市最大的藏传佛教寺院。原为清世宗胤禛即位前的府邸。胤禛继承王位后，将其变为皇家行宫，1725 年定名为雍和宫。1744 年改为藏传佛教格鲁派寺院。

寺院由雍和宫大殿、永佑殿、法轮殿、万福阁等组成，占地 66400 平方米。万福阁又称大佛楼，正中供奉举世闻名的白檀香木雕弥勒佛像。该佛像高 26 米，其中 8 米深埋地下，直径 8 米，总重量约 100 吨，是中国最大独木雕佛像。雍和宫内藏珍宝无数，常年香火不断，这里不仅是京城的佛教圣地，也是汉、满、蒙、藏文化艺术丰富的宝库。

143. The Wanfu Tower in the Yonghegong Lamasery is a combination of the Han and Tibetan architectural styles. (Photo by Du Dianwen)
雍和宫万福阁是集汉、藏等风格为一体的建筑物。（杜殿文 摄）

143

144. The Falun (Wheel of the Law) Hall.
(Photo by Du Dianwen)
法轮殿内景。（杜殿文 摄）

The shrine built of golden-striped Nanmu hard-
145. wood in the Zhaofo Tower is one of the three
best-carved wooden items in the Yonghegong
Lama-sery. (Photo by Du Dianwen)
雍和宫内木雕三绝之一 "昭佛楼的金丝楠木佛龛"。
（杜殿文 摄）

	145
144	

法輪殿

6. The *Canon of the Great White Canopy* written in gold ink is a major scripture of Esoteric Buddhism.
(Photo by Du Dianwen)
用金汁书写的《大白伞盖经》，为藏传佛教密乘主要经典。
（杜殿文 摄）

7. A traditional Buddhist dance performed by monks in the Yonghegong Lamasery.
宫内举行传统的跳羌姆佛事活动。

8. The 26-m-high wooden Buddhist statue has been included in the *Guinness Book of Records*.
(Photo by Du Dianwen)
26 米高的木雕大佛像已载入吉尼斯世界纪录。
（杜殿文 摄）

Situated in Huangsi Street, outside the old Deshengmen city gate of Beijing, the temple was founded by the Fifth Dalai Lama during the Qing Dynasty. The Sixth Panchen Lama meditated and taught here in 1780. In memory of the Sixth Panchen Lama, Emperor Qianlong built a stupa to enshrine the holy man's hat and robes in 1782, and named it the Qingjinghuacheng Stupa. Covering a floor space of 15,000 sq m, the temple has 59 halls and accommodation for monks. In September 1987, the Tenth Panchen Erdeni Chokyi Gyaltsen inaugurated the China Tibetan-Language Academy of Buddhism at the Xihuangsi Temple, which has since then become the cradle of senior students of Tibetan Buddhism in China.

位于北京德胜门外黄寺大街。该寺是清王朝为五世达赖喇嘛所建，1780年又成为六世班禅安禅说法之场所。1782年乾隆皇帝为纪念六世班禅，在此建造六世班禅衣冠塔，称清净化城塔。该寺建筑面积1.5万多平方米，有殿堂房舍59间。1987年9月第十世班禅额尔德尼·确吉坚赞在此创办中国藏语系高级佛学院，使西黄寺成为培养藏传佛教高级佛学人才的摇篮。

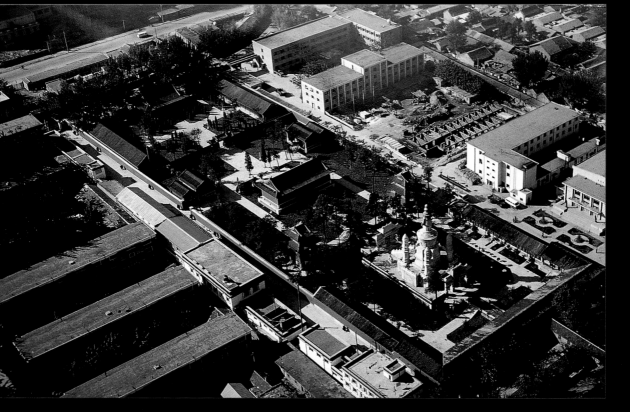

149. A full view of the Xihuangsi
    Temple.
    (Photo by Zhang Zhaoji)
    西黄寺全景。（张肇基　摄）
150. The main hall of the
    Xihuangsi Temple.
    寺内大殿。
151. The Qingjinghuacheng Stupa.
    (Photo by Du Dianwen)
    六世班禅的衣冠塔—清净化城塔。
    （杜殿文　摄）

	150	
149		151

152. Acolytes of the China Tibetan-
     Language Academy of Buddhism.
     高级佛学院僧人。

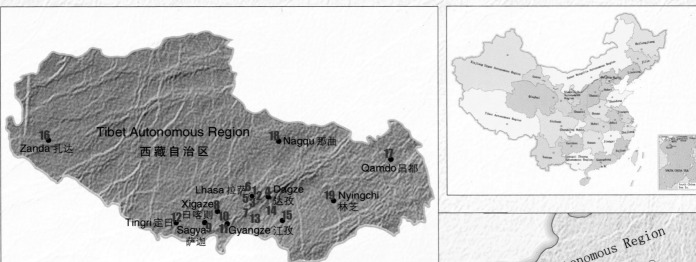

Tibet Autonomous Region
西藏自治区

16 Zanda 扎达

18 Nagqu 那曲

17 Qamdo 昌都

19 Nyingchi 林芝

Lhasa 拉萨
Dagze 达孜
Xigaze 日喀则
Tingri 定日
Sagya 萨迦
Gyangze 江孜

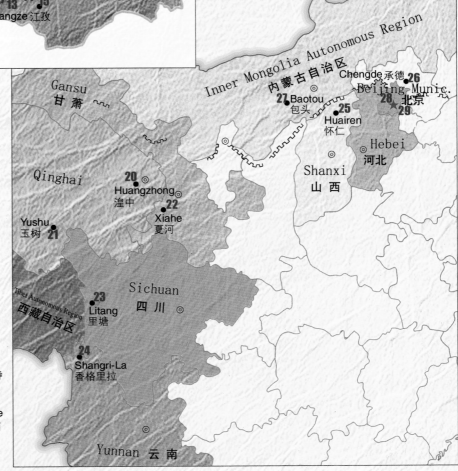

Gansu 甘肃

Qinghai

Inner Mongolia Autonomous Region
内蒙古自治区

Chengde 承德 26
Beijing Munic. 北京
27 Baotou 包头
25 Huairen 怀仁
28
29

Hebei 河北

Shanxi 山西

20 Huangzhong 湟中
22 Xiahe 夏河

Yushu 玉树 21

Sichuan 四川

Tibet Autonomous Region
西藏自治区

23 Litang 里塘

24 Shangri-La 香格里拉

Yunnan 云南

1. The Potala Palace 布达拉宫
2. The Jokhang Temple 大昭寺
3. The Ramoche Temple 小昭寺
4. The Ganden Monastery 甘丹寺
5. The Drepung Monastery 哲蚌寺
6. The Sera Monastery 色拉寺
7. The Tsurpu Monastery 楚布寺
8. The Tashilhunpo Monastery 扎什伦布寺
9. The Sakya Monastery 萨迦寺
10. The Shalu Monastery 夏鲁寺
11. The Pelkor Chode Monastery 白居寺
12. The Rongpo Monastery 绒布寺
13. The Samye Monastery 桑耶寺
14. The Trandruk Monastery 昌珠寺
15. The Yumbulagang 雍布拉康
16. The Toling Monastery 托林寺
17. The Champa Ling 强巴林寺
18. The Shabten Monastery 孝登寺
19. The Lama Ling 喇嘛林寺
20. The Kumbum Monastery 塔尔寺
21. The Kyegu Monastery 结古寺
22. The Labrang Monastery 拉卜楞寺
23. The Chamchen Chokhor Monastery 长青春科尔寺
24. The Ganden Songtsen Ling 噶丹·松赞林寺
25. Temples on Mount Wutai 五台山
26. The Eight Outlying Temples Surrounding the
    Chengde Imperial Summer Resort 承德外八庙
27. The Wudangzhao Monastery 五当召
28. The Yonghegong Lamasery 雍和宫
29. The Xihuangsi Temple 西黄寺

图书在版编目（CIP）数据

中国藏传佛教寺庙／成卫东编． —北京：外文出版社，2003.12
ISBN 7-119-03347-6

Ⅰ．中… Ⅱ.成… Ⅲ.喇嘛教－寺庙－简介－中国－英、汉 Ⅳ.B947.2
中国版本图书馆 CIP 数据核字(2003)第 055067 号

编　　撰：成卫东
摄　　影：成卫东
选题策划：兰佩瑾
翻　　译：郁　苓
英文核稿：梁良兴
设　　计：元　青
责任编辑：兰佩瑾

中国藏传佛教寺庙

© 外文出版社
外文出版社出版
（中国北京百万庄大街24号）
邮政编码：100037
外文出版社网页: http://www.flp.com.cn
外文出版社电子邮件地址: info@flp.com.cn
　　　　　　　　 sales@flp.com.cn
天时包装(深圳)有限公司承印
中国国际图书贸易总公司发行
（中国北京车公庄西路35号）
北京邮政信箱第 399 号 邮政编码100044 作
2004 年(20开)第一版
2004 年第一版第一次印刷
（英汉）
ISBN 7-119-03347-6/J·1654(外)
009900（平）
85-EC-564S